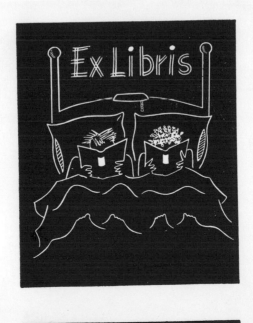

MR. INCREDIBLE

MR. INCREDIBLE

A STORY ABOUT AUTISM,
OVERCOMING CHALLENGING BEHAVIOR,
AND A FAMILY'S FIGHT
FOR SPECIAL EDUCATION RIGHTS

THE ORP LIBRARY

WRITTEN BY
JEFF KRUKAR, PH.D.
CHELSEA McCUTCHIN
WITH
JAMES G. BALESTRIERI

rtc Publishing

WRITERS OF THE ROUND TABLE PRESS
PO BOX 511
HIGHLAND PARK, IL 60035

Publisher	COREY MICHAEL BLAKE
Executive Editor	KATIE GUTIERREZ
Post Production	DAVID CHARLES COHEN
Directoress of Happiness	ERIN COHEN
Director of Author Services	KRISTIN WESTBERG
Facts Keeper	MIKE WINICOUR
Front Cover Design	ANALEE PAZ
Interior Design and Layout	SUNNY DIMARTINO
Proofreading	RITA HESS
Last Looks	JESS PLACE
Digital Book Conversion	SUNNY DIMARTINO
Digital Publishing	SUNNY DIMARTINO

Printed in the United States of America
First Edition: March 2013
10 9 8 7 6 5 4 3 2

Library of Congress Cataloging-in-Publication Data
Krukar, Jeff
Mr. incredible: a story about autism, overcoming challenging behavior,
and a family's fight for special education rights / Jeff Krukar and
Chelsea McCutchin with James G. Balestrieri.—1st ed. p. cm.
Print ISBN: 978-1-939418-14-2   Digital ISBN: 978-1-939418-15-9
Library of Congress Control Number: 2013935244
Number 5 in the series: The ORP Library
The ORP Library: Mr. Incredible

RTC Publishing is an imprint of Writers of the Round Table, Inc.
Writers of the Round Table Press and the RTC Publishing logo
are trademarks of Writers of the Round Table, Inc.

CONTENTS

INTRODUCTION

Today, according to the U.S. Department of Health and Human Services, more than 5.5 million children—or eight percent of kids—in the U.S. have some form of disability. Whether the problem is physical, behavioral, or emotional, these children struggle to communicate, learn, and relate to others. While there is no longer *segregation* in the same sense as there was in the 1950s, what remains the same is the struggle. Even with all of our resources and technology, parents of children with disabilities fight battles every day to find the help and education their children need.

I have led Oconomowoc Residential Programs (ORP) for almost thirty years. We're a family of companies offering specialized services and care for children, adolescents, and adults with disabilities. Too often, when parents of children with disabilities try to find funding for programs like ours, they are bombarded by red tape, conflicting information, or no information at all, so they struggle blindly for years to secure an appropriate education. Meanwhile, home life, and the child's wellbeing, suffers. In cases when parents and caretakers have exhausted their options—and their hope—ORP is here to help. We felt it was time to offer parents a new, unexpected tool to fight back: stories that educate, empower, and inspire.

The original idea was to create a library of comic books that could empower families with information to reclaim their rights. We wanted to give parents and caretakers the information they need to advocate for themselves, as well as provide educators and therapists with a therapeutic tool. And, of course, we wanted to reach the children—to offer them a visual representation of their journey that would show that they aren't alone, nor are they wrong or "bad" for their differences. What we found in the process of writing original stories for the comics is that these journeys are too long, too complex, to be contained within a standard comic. So what we are now creating is an ORP library of disabilities books—traditional books geared toward parents, caretakers, educators, and therapists, *and* comic books portraying the world through the eyes of children with disabilities. Both styles of books share what we have learned while advocating for families over the years while also honestly highlighting their emotional journeys. We're creating communication devices that anyone can read to understand complex disabilities in a new way.

In an ideal situation, these books will be used therapeutically, to communicate the message, and to help support the work ORP and companies like ours are doing. The industry has changed dramatically and is not likely to turn around any time soon—certainly not without more people being aware of families' struggles. We have an opportunity to put a face to the conversation, reach out to families, and start that dialogue.

Caring for children with disabilities consumes your life. We know that. And we want you to realize, through these stories, that you are not alone. We can help.

Sincerely,
Jim Balestrieri
CEO, Oconomowoc Residential Programs
www.orplibrary.com

A NOTE ABOUT THIS BOOK

Autism spectrum disorder is a complex syndrome that affects children in different ways. The child with autism spectrum disorder depicted in the following story struggles with significant emotional and behavioral difficulties that require a therapeutic environment. The great majority of children with autism spectrum disorder do not resemble the child shown in this story. But those who do resemble him face challenges that have made it difficult to benefit from education in the public school system. At Genesee Lake School, we strive to build relationships with the children in our care so that they learn new skills that will lead to a successful return to their home, school, and community. It is our hope that the following story will add to your own understanding of the often lonely journey experienced by families with children with these unique challenges and gifts.

PROLOGUE
AT HIS OWN PACE

Elena Phillips pulled her long, dark hair into a bun. She twisted her fingers around the knot and wrapped an elastic band to secure it as she left the break room. Her heels clicked as she strode down the hallway to gather her purse from her locker and clock out for the day. As the head manager of a major department store, her job wasn't without its challenges, and while she loved it, she was relieved to clock out a little early after the big weekend she'd had.

"Hey, Elena!" she heard her co-manager, Alicia call out. "So sorry we couldn't make it to Adam's birthday party this weekend. Someone had to hold down the fort here!"

Elena smiled as she lied to her coworker. "If it was anything like last weekend, I think you had the harder job."

Alicia laughed. "Possibly so. I wanted to catch you and give you this, though." She handed Elena a blue bag with a rattle and a big, glittery ONE across the front.

"That's so thoughtful!" Elena exclaimed. "Thank you. I'm sure he'll love it."

"I included a gift receipt, just in case it doesn't fit. Are you heading out now?"

"Yeah. I'm taking him to his one-year appointment with the pediatrician today."

"Poor guy, those shots are killer. I hope the gift makes

him smile, at least. I'm sure his party was a huge success."

"Sure was. See you tomorrow!" Elena fished her keys from her purse and walked away from Alicia before tears could make her brown eyes shine brighter. She'd tried to make Adam's birthday party fun for everyone. She'd invited all of their family for a pool party. Adam loved the water, and having been born in April, the Florida weather required a way to keep cool.

The day had started out great. Elena flipped on the television to Saturday morning cartoons while they engaged in a "family cuddle," one of her older daughter Shannon's favorite things to do. It was one of Elena's favorites, too, as it typically brought her another half hour of sleep. Afterward, she made silver-dollar pancakes for breakfast, and Shannon, who was almost three, had given Adam the gift she'd picked out for him—a set of big LEGO DUPLO blocks. Shannon's light brown pigtails bounced as the children spread the blocks out on the living room floor while Elena worked on braiding the streamers in the kitchen.

"No, Adam," Shannon said. "Stack the blocks, like this."

Curious, Elena peeked around the corner and saw that Adam was just staring at an orange block, his chubby fingers grasping it like a lifeline. When Shannon tried to pull the block from Adam's hand and guide it to the tower she was working on, Adam screamed as though she'd hurt him.

Elena rushed into the room to comfort her baby, but he only continued screaming when she picked him up. She could smell the syrup on his hot breath as he wailed right into her face. She chided Shannon, telling her that it was Adam's birthday and his present, and they had to play his way today. She put the block back into Adam's hand, but he only flung it across the room, and soon the sound of Shannon's cries filled the room. The noise made Adam's body tense further, escalating his mood. Elena sighed, pulling her daughter into her lap, too, and closed her eyes for a moment. She never knew that having two small children could be so overwhelming.

"Daddy!" Shannon cried, jumping up from Elena's lap.

Elena opened her eyes to see her sleepy husband standing in the entrance to the living room.

"Sorry we woke you," she said. "It's just . . ."

Jon was a mechanic at UPS who worked overnight shifts. He was trying to rest before the party that afternoon, but the commotion must have stirred him.

"I'm fine," he called over Adam's screaming. "Everything okay out here? What's wrong, Bubba?" Jon scooped Shannon into his arms as walked over to Elena, who was holding Adam on the floor. Adam hadn't stopped his ear-piercing shrieks except to catch his breath.

Elena shrugged at Jon as she wrapped her arms all the way around her son, squeezing him gently. Finally, Adam yielded to her chest. She had work to do, so after a few minutes of steady calm, she slipped him into the Ergo, a baby carrier that would keep him close to her while she finished preparations for his party.

The afternoon was much the same: Adam cried when his family members passed him around, and the only smile Jon caught on the many pictures he took was when Adam was splashing in the water with his mother. When Elena lit the candle on his little cake and everyone starting singing "Happy Birthday," Adam's face crumpled and he fell apart. The screaming didn't stop until the house was quiet again and Elena had him in the bathtub.

"Well, that was different than Shannon's first birthday," Jon remarked as he knelt down by the bathtub with his wife.

"She squealed and laughed when we sang happy birthday," Elena remembered, wistfully running her lathered fingers through Adam's hair, which was dark and thick with coarse curls. "Everyone commented on that belly laugh that was bigger than she was. I think I'm going to bring this up to the pediatrician next week."

Elena snapped back from her memories of the weekend and into the present as she pulled into her in-laws' driveway to pick up her son. She was lucky—George and Penny were the kind of people who were destined to be grandparents. They happily kept the children whenever her work schedule overlapped with Jon's. She removed her seatbelt and took a moment to breathe before leaving her car and ringing the doorbell. From inside, she heard Shannon exclaim, "Mommy!" as George and Penny's Boston terrier zapped and scurried across the tile foyer. A second later, Adam started screaming across the house. The sound got closer as her mother-in-law answered the door with a red-faced, snotty Adam on her hip.

"What's wrong, little guy?" Elena took her son from Penny's arms.

"I just had him calmed down when the doorbell rang and all hell broke loose again," Penny said, flustered as she tried to smooth her normally perfect short haircut. She was petite, and although she'd grown a bit round since becoming a grandmother, she maintained her appearance as if she were still the flight attendant she had been in her twenties. "He's been like this all morning. Kind of like his birthday party."

Elena held her son close to her while her daughter hugged her legs. She reached down and patted Shannon's head while trying to console Adam. "I'm taking Adam to the doctor, sweetheart," she told Shannon, bending down to meet her daughter's green eyes. Her honey-brown hair flipped out of the pigtails that Penny had painstakingly French braided that morning. Physically, she was a little Elena, but she'd inherited her father's fair coloring. "You're going to stay with Grammy for another hour or so. Then, when I come back to get you, we'll all go get ice cream before heading home. Sound good?"

"Yes, Mommy." Shannon retreated to her grandmother, and Penny smiled and wished Elena luck at the doctor's office. As the door closed, Elena heard Shannon ask if they could play tea party.

Half an hour later, Elena caught her reflection in the two-way mirror hanging over the pediatric exam table. Her skin was still youthful, but she wondered if her eyes always looked this tired. While the doctor was looking over Adam, she realized that she never really looked at herself anymore. Her morning routine had become automatic: she brushed out her hair and flat ironed any stray pieces that were starting to give way to the Florida humidity. Then she applied rudimentary foundation, eye shadow, and mascara. She dabbed on a bit of lip gloss in the car on the way to work—all without examining her face. She couldn't say why, but the realization was saddening.

"Looks like you have a healthy little guy, Elena." Dr. Peterson smiled underneath his grey moustache. He was a longtime friend of Elena's family who had treated her when she was a little girl. He was naturally the doctor she chose for her own children.

"He is doing well, physically," Elena agreed. "I'm a little worried about him, though. He's done nothing but scream lately. He freaked out at his birthday party this weekend, and his tantrums are getting worse. I was filling out the questionnaire before the appointment, and I realized that I can't even tell you if he's babbling because he screams so much." Elena was apprehensive about his response; even mentioning these things to him took a lot from her. She didn't want to give power to the concern that her child was anything but absolutely perfect—although that concern was growing each day. "At this age, Shannon was . . ."

"Boys are walkers, girls are talkers," Dr. Peterson interrupted, smiling. "You can't compare your children, Elena. So, you really don't hear him making babbling noises?"

"Well, he does slightly when he's on his own. Like he's in his own little world and just kind of yayayayay-aying. He doesn't respond to me when I call his name, though. Most of the time he doesn't even look up. It's . . . disconcerting." Elena remembered the many times she had called Adam's name, expecting to see his eyes lift to hers, some hint of recognition, one of those delightful baby smiles—but nothing. It was as if she weren't in the room—as if he didn't even realize she was his mother.

She looked over at her son, who was banging the cardboard-paged books Dr. Peterson kept in his patient rooms against the side of the two-way mirror. Adam showed no interest in the books' illustrations of a hungry caterpillar and a brown bear, nor had he even noticed his reflection in the mirror. Elena remembered Shannon's one-year appointment—when she'd had to keep her from "giving the other baby kisses," simply because this was a doctor's office and she wasn't sure what kinds of germs were resting on the surface. Shannon and Adam were definitely different at this age.

"I understand your concerns," Dr. Peterson said, "but I think he's fine. You were blessed with a bright daughter as a first child, and your son is moving at his own pace. Shannon is a talker," he added with a laugh. "I bet Adam feels like he can't get a word in edgewise."

"Maybe," Elena said, unconvinced. She gathered up Adam and her diaper bag. She wanted Dr. Peterson's words to comfort her, but her stomach was still tangled with anxiety. "So there's nothing we should be doing? No . . . tests or evaluations?"

Dr. Peterson jotted a note on Adam's record. "I don't think so. Just keep an eye on him, and let's talk again at his eighteen-month appointment."

Jon was on the couch when Elena got home with the children.

"My monkeys!" he called as he jumped up and came in the foyer to grab both children and throw them over his shoulder.

Shannon was hysterical with giggles. Adam just looked around, upside down on his father's back.

"What did the good doctor say?" Jon asked his wife, leaning in for a quick peck.

"He says all is well. I told him about the birthday party and that my gut says something isn't right. He just said we'd check again at eighteen months if things are the same."

"Things won't be the same in six months. You'll see. My parents told me I was slower at some things, too." Jon sat on the floor and swung his children into his lap, where Shannon snuggled on his chest and Adam struggled to get away. When Jon let his son go, he wandered to the front door and ran his fingers over the keyhole on the knob.

PART I

CHAPTER 1
A LIGHT WENT OFF

Six months later, Elena took Adam back to Dr. Peterson's office. Although Adam had continued babbling to himself, the only marked improvement Elena had seen in her son was the reoccurrence of the word "Mim." Elena knew that he was trying to say *Mom*, even though he wasn't consistently making eye contact with anyone. The family praised Adam for his speech, having an impromptu dance party each time he uttered the word. Still, Elena had found a developmental checklist online and printed it out to discuss her concerns with Dr. Peterson. She felt armed with not only her intuition but also with written proof that something was off with Adam. While he excelled at all the physical milestones listed—able to run and scribble, for example—he didn't hit any of the sensory and cognitive markers. He wasn't showing affection, wouldn't sit still for a story, and certainly wasn't saying ten words.

"How's that big boy today?" Dr. Peterson walked into the exam room wearing a big smile. His booming voice echoed over the tile floor, causing Adam to jump and whine. "Sorry, buddy," Dr. Peterson got close to Adam to

3

apologize when the full-on wailing began.

Elena grabbed her son and told the doctor, "This is what I'm talking about. Your voice scares the hell out of him, but he won't look at me when I call his name. I printed this checklist. He's . . ."

"Let's see what's going on." Dr. Peterson leaned in to examine Adam on his mother's lap. After checking his ears and throat, the doctor struggled to listen to his heartbeat as Adam protested with loud wailing. "I know you don't like it, big guy. I know. Mama's got you. You're fine." Dr. Peterson tried to comfort Adam with his voice, but still Adam bucked and fought the doctor's hands. When he completed the examination, Dr. Peterson handed Adam a tongue depressor, which Adam looked at for a moment before hurling it across the room. Elena pulled him close to her, whispering in his ear, "We don't throw, Adam." He calmed at her touch but wiggled down to get to the Matchbox cars that were across the room. She looked up at the doctor, her look conveying her frustration.

"He's a little stubborn. Elena," Dr. Peterson said. "I've been doing this since before you were born. I've seen all kinds of children, and Adam is just a late bloomer. He'll get there. Keep working with him. It might be a good idea to enroll him in daycare instead of allowing him to stay home with his grandmother. The interaction with other kids his age might encourage him to come out of his shell a little."

Elena was indignant. Dr. Peterson hadn't even looked at her checklist. "Well, then—boys will be boys, I guess," she said crisply, ending the appointment.

In the next six months, Adam's babbling stopped, but the screaming got worse. It was as though a light went off in her son's eyes. Elena couldn't quite put her finger on the when or the why, but where recognition had clicked before, now there was nothing. The only things replacing the long periods of silence were seemingly random outbursts with tears and screams and violent thrashing. The days when Elena was home with her son, she found herself putting on the same VHS of *Barney*, fighting to get him to eat anything other than spaghetti. The only reprieve from his relentless tantrums was the pool, where she played with her children for hours. He was a different person in the water, where he would glide the three feet from the steps to his mother's arms. For all of his verbal incapability, he was so physically able that it was hard to believe he wasn't even two.

One evening after dinner, Elena had her children in the bathtub when Adam was lining up his Hot Wheels on the side of the tub. Shannon turned to her brother. "Adam, you're not playing with those right." She took two off the side of the tub and started making a racetrack on the other side. Adam went ballistic, shrieking so loudly his face turned a mottled purplish. His cries were only interrupted by the *thump* when he banged his head against the shower wall.

"Adam, no!" Elena cried, pulling her son from the tub and wrapping his slippery body in a towel. He grunted and struggled with her until she was finally able to swaddle the entire towel around him and get a grip on his torso. "Adam! Adam! Look at me, buddy." Adam had calmed, but his big brown eyes were still staring at the ceiling over Elena's shoulder.

CHAPTER 2
HANDFUL

The next morning, Elena had a district visit from her supervisor, Jackie. Unlike most of her colleagues, she didn't mind these pop-in visits, and her store always did quite well. After reviewing the sales numbers, Jackie looked up at Elena.

"Good work, Elena. We wanted to let you know that your hard work doesn't go unnoticed."

"Well, thanks."

"You took this store from non-performing to over-performing. You've shaped up the staff, and the numbers reflect your success. I wasn't going to talk with you about this until after our summer sale, but I wanted to let you know that I'm moving up. The Orlando market is considerably bigger, and they need me there. That means there will be a vacancy at my job . . ." A smile teased the corners of Jackie's lips. "And I was wondering if you'd be interested."

"Really?" Elena couldn't believe it. She'd worked for this company since she was a part-time seasonal associate her senior year of high school. She'd dreamed of becoming a district manager but thought it would take longer than ten years to get there.

Elena left work on cloud nine. She went home to share her good news with Jon before picking up the kids, only to find her mother-in-law and her children at her house with her husband. She was perplexed when she walked in, as Jon was normally sleeping at this time and the kids were at their grandmother's house. They were sitting in the living room while Shannon and Adam watched a video on the floor.

"Elena, you're home," Penny greeted her daughter-in-law.

"Yes. I was going to throw some potatoes in the oven for dinner before coming to get the kids. What's going on?"

Jon gestured for his wife to come sit next to him on the couch. She sat, with trepidation. "So . . ." Jon started, "Adam had one of his temper tantrums again today. Not only did he break Grandma Rose's vase, he . . . just show her, Mom."

Penny lifted her sleeve to show Elena where her forearm was a deep purple bruise surrounded by eight perfect teeth marks.

"Oh my God!" Elena cried, horrified. She reached out to touch the tender flesh around the bite. "Are you okay?"

"Fine. However, I—" Penny's voice cracked. "I don't think I can keep up with him anymore. You know how much I love him, but his tantrums—"

"I know," Elena said hurriedly. She forced a smile. "I know. It's okay."

Elena couldn't fault Penny. She knew what a handful Adam could be, and if *she* wasn't sure how to deal with it, she couldn't expect Penny to. She turned to Jon. "Did you make him apologize?" Although Adam couldn't speak, Elena and Jon had been working with him on gentle touches and hugs for apologies. Elena was convinced that nonverbal didn't mean totally noncommunicative; Adam could still show he was sorry.

Jon looked sheepish. "I tried . . ."

"No just trying. We have to be tougher on him. He can't get away with treating his grandmother this way! Adam! Adam!"

From the front of the room, Shannon whipped her head around to her mother's voice, but Adam continued watching the purple dinosaur dance across the screen, seemingly oblivious to the scene around him.

CHAPTER 3
DESPERATE FOR ANSWERS

"I don't know what to do!" Elena exclaimed at Dr. Peterson. She'd scheduled Adam's two-year check-up early to address his worsening issues. While she was starting to question the competence of the doctor she'd been seeing for almost thirty years, time constraints and loyalty prevented her from moving on. After explaining that Adam was no longer babbling at all, that he had yet to say a "real" word, and the violence with which he was acting out—biting was becoming more and more common—Elena was desperate for answers. She looked at Adam on the exam table just as he jumped off and fell to his knees.

"Adam! Buddy, are you okay?" Elena fell to a crouch, reaching to pick Adam up. He didn't respond—only squirmed from Elena's grasp to try climbing the table again. Dr. Peterson looked concerned but stepped back to see how Elena handled this. She set Adam back up on the table but kept her hand on his belly so he couldn't do it again. She handed him a board book, but he threw the book at her face and screamed. When she tried to hold him, the screaming only intensified. She turned back to the doctor, making strong eye contact. Adam's screams were such a part of her life that she had learned to conduct conversations around them.

"Do you see what I'm talking about?" she asked. "Absolutely no response to my voice and what I tell him to do. No looking me in the eye when I talk to him. No . . . anything but *this*." She gestured to her screaming child, his face mottled an angry purple from forcing the shrieks out from deep in his belly. "I don't know what this is, but it isn't just *stubbornness*."

Dr. Peterson sighed, rubbing the bridge of his nose. Adam's screeches were piercing. "Listen, I'd like to make a referral to a pediatric audiologist to check his hearing. Though I don't think that's the problem, it's possible that he's not registering your voice or tone, which of course would affect his own language abilities, and if he's in any pain, that could contribute to the tantrums." Dr. Peterson scribbled on his pad. "In the meantime, though, you might want to consider disciplining him differently. Have you read *The Happiest Toddler on the Block*? I highly recommend it to all parents who have similar issues with their children."

"Let's see what the hearing results are, and we'll go from there," Elena replied curtly. She'd known Dr. Peterson her whole life, but *disciplining him differently*? Really?

She brought Adam home, where Jon and Shannon were playing pony—one of Shannon's favorite games—on the living room floor. Sitting on Jon's back, she gently kicked her feet into her father's ribs. "Ya! Pony! Take me to Mommy and Adam!"

Jon neighed and reared up to buck Shannon playfully. Her giggles filled the room as Elena set down her bags and slumped onto the couch for a few minutes before she had to change clothes and go to work. Shannon jumped off her father's back and ran to her brother. She led him by the hand into their playroom, happy to have him home again.

"What's the verdict?" Jon asked, sitting up.

"He wants to do a hearing test. I know that's not the problem—he jumps at loud noises, and they sometimes set him off. But at least we're doing something and we can rule hearing out." Elena sighed. "We have an appointment on Thursday morning. I'm closing that night, so we should be fine."

Jon echoed Elena's sigh. "So that means I'll have another day this week with no sleep. Great."

"I'm doing the best I can, Jon." Elena tried to keep her voice soft and loving. She didn't have the strength to fight. Without childcare from her mother-in-law, she and Jon were trying to match their schedules as much as possible. That often meant that one them was utterly exhausted—sometimes both of them. Adding insult to injury, Elena had to turn down the offer of the district manager position. She'd worked so hard to get there, but the travel and long hours just weren't feasible with her current situation.

Friday morning, Jackie walked into the store unannounced. Elena was with a customer, but as soon as she could excuse herself from the floor, she went back to the office, where Jackie was setting up her laptop.

"What's going on?" Elena asked.

Jackie smiled back at her. "I have an interview here today."

"Who?"

"Alicia. Since you turned down the DM position, we were scrambling to think of someone who could fill it. Then, it hit me. If I can't have you, why not your right-hand-woman? I talked to Alicia the other day when you were off, and we agreed to meet today for an interview before her shift starts." Jackie's voice reflected genuine excitement at the prospect of promoting Elena's co-manager.

"That's great!" Elena tried to mirror Jackie's excitement, but she knew that *she* was the one who'd earned that job. "I'll let her know you're back here when she gets in."

"Elena, you have a call on line three," an associate's voice echoed over the loudspeaker.

Eyebrows knit in bafflement, Elena picked up the phone. It was Dr. Peterson.

"I hope you don't mind that I called you at work."

"Not at all. I hope you have some news."

"I do, and it's all good! The nurse from the pediatric audiologist called my office. Adam is a completely hearing child. He's no different than Shannon was or than you were at his age."

"Okay . . ." Elena twisted the cord around her finger. "That's great news. But where does that leave us in regards to his behavior?"

"Were you able to pick up that book I recommended at our last visit?"

Elena sighed in frustration. Was she not making herself clear enough? As much as she didn't want to admit that anything wasn't perfect about her son, she was craving answers. She'd read up on developmental milestones enough to know what to ask for, specifically. "I don't think so. Dr. Peterson—I'd like to get him checked out for a language disorder."

In the last week or so, Elena had spent her free time on the computer, visiting parenting websites and searching lists of Adam's symptoms with the hope of finding an explanation for what was happening. She found a website for the Speech-Language-Hearing Association, which talked about receptive and expressive language disorders. By now, Adam should not only be saying simple words (*mama, dada, toy, dog*), he should be able to string those simple words together into short sentences and questions, identify parts of his body, and generally show a curiosity to interact with others. It galled her to think Dr. Peterson wanted to ignore all the signs.

The doctor was silent for a moment. Finally, he sighed. "Okay. If it'll make you feel better, I know a great speech and language pathologist. She can come to your home and work with him. Her name is Lyndsey Wallace. I'll have her office give you a call to set up an appointment."

"That would be great. Thank you, Dr. Peterson."

She clicked the phone down and let her hand linger on the headset for just a moment. *Language disorder.* As many times as the words had run through her mind, as many times as she'd reread the information she'd printed out, as many times as she had lost sleep thinking about this, she'd never given voice to the specific fear. Her stomach was sick, and she felt as though she'd given something away that she really should have kept.

CHAPTER 4
BIRTH TO THREE

"Hello, Adam, look at what I have!" Lyndsey Wallace's voice echoed. One of her favorite warm ups was working with a play farm. The back of the toy had a grain silo that echoed nicely, and playing with it typically engaged children easily and encouraged communication. Lyndsey picked up the farm, turned, and saw Adam busy lining up his Hot Wheels on the rug.

"Adam, look at what I have here! Look! Doesn't this farm door sound silly when it opens?" Lyndsey was careful not to touch the boy, only to try to engage him verbally. She switched play activities. "Adam, I really like cars. Can I play with your cars, too?" She grabbed a car from the bucket and starting making *vroom* noises with it. "Is this a race car?"

Adam continued looking down at the cars and did not respond to Lyndsey's voice, or affect. It was as though Lyndsey weren't even there.

Elena slid down from the couch and onto the floor. "This is what I mean. He obviously enjoys the cars in some way, so I bought him this huge collection and box for the cars, a rug that is decorated with roads. I've tried playing with him the way you are now. But he's going on two and a half, and I'm not sure he gets how to play with others. He just doesn't seem to care." Her face fell.

Lyndsey saw this with parents of many of her clients. Pediatricians were more likely to recommend speech therapy than anything else, and she was the first person to see children with an autism spectrum disorder before they were finally diagnosed. Although she was not qualified to diagnose an autism spectrum disorder, she was able to recognize some of the signs and symptoms. In the brief observation of Adam, she saw that he wasn't able to engage in pretend play, and he displayed no eye contact. The most troubling thing was that he didn't try to get Lyndsey to see what he saw, or create a shared experience. Clinicians often assessed this capacity for "joint attention" in children. Most two-year-olds drive their parents crazy trying to show them their toys, clothes, and food—everything in their brand new world. Adam didn't seem to care if Lyndsey saw his cars or not.

Lyndsey realized it was only her first session, but it was important to give the parents some additional guidance. She chose her words carefully for Elena, who watched with dread in her eyes. "This is only our first session," Lyndsey said. "I'm an unfamiliar person, and he still has to get used to me. What I'm seeing here, though—is it similar to what you see every day as far as the play and lack of response to others?"

"Yes," Elena said, sighing. "It's like this every day."

"Have you thought about getting involved with Birth to Three?"

"I don't know what Birth to Three is exactly," Elena replied.

"It's a program run by the county. Their services are free to families with concerns about their children who are under three years old. They'll provide you with a complete evaluation and also pay for my sessions, so that your insurance doesn't have to." Lyndsey paused. "They'll also provide Adam with any additional therapies should he need them."

Impulsively, Elena reached over and hugged Lyndsey. She was so relieved that *someone* was finally taking her concerns seriously. The suggestion of Birth to Three finally gave her a proactive avenue to pursue to help her child.

A week later, Elena and Jon met with Miguel, a caseworker for the county's Birth to Three program, along with another speech therapist and an occupational therapist. They sat in the Phillipses' living room as an engrossed Adam watched *Barney* from the floor.

"It's important that you're as much a part of this evaluation as possible. We want to see Adam comfortable and at his best, so we will do a lot of the evaluation in the house. We also know that you'll catch things that we miss, so we're going to ask you a lot of questions. After all, you know him best." Miguel smiled at the Phillipses.

The evaluation began with the occupational therapist asking Adam to help him stack a set of blocks into a tower. Adam ignored the OT and Miguel, wanting to throw the blocks, and when the OT became more persistent and talked louder, Adam wailed and banged his head on the tile floor. Elena rushed to pick him up, but Jon got there first. When Jon picked him up, Adam head butted his father right in the nose.

"Jon!" Elena exclaimed as a rush of dark red dripped

from her husband's nose onto Adam's head.

Jon lifted a hand to his nose, pulling it away to see the blood. He winced, seeing stars for a few seconds before his son quieted and his body relaxed. "Well, I'm going to get cleaned up. We're glad you're here." Jon excused himself, leaving a calm Adam on the floor and a tearful Elena on the couch.

A few days later, Elena and Jon met Miguel in his office.

"Adam's a great kid," he said, smiling.

"I agree," Elena said. "I sense there's a 'but' coming."

"No 'but,' I promise," Miguel said. "Now, Adam does meet the criteria for Birth to Three services, at a twenty-five percent delay in language, cognition, self-help, and social emotional development. We've put together an individualized family service plan that lays out what *we're* going to do and what *you're* going to do. We're all going to work together to help Adam as much as we can. He's only six months away from turning three, at which point we'll have to make sure a special education referral is made to the local school district. But I promise that we will do as much as we can to get him ready for that transition." He handed a packet over to Jon and Elena, who gathered close together to look at the information.

"This looks a little intimidating, and it covers a lot of material, but I'll help break it down for you. The plan covers eight main areas. The first paragraph identifies Adam's present levels of development. You can see that he is on target physically, but is behind in language, cognition, self-help, and social emotional development. In the second paragraph, we've identified your resources, which include your health insurance and time commitments, as well as the priorities and concerns that you laid out for me in our initial interview—mostly that Adam is still nonverbal and is prone to aggressive attacks that have become increasingly frequent. We'd like to work with him and your family on these concerns. The third paragraph shows the outcomes we expect in the next six months. For example, we'd like to see Adam saying three words and showing a decrease in his self-injurious behavior, such as banging his head against the walls or floor. We'll also be working with Lyndsey, your speech therapist, along with Bruce, an occupational therapist. Starting next week, Adam will see each provider three times a week for thirty-minute sessions. These services will last until we have achieved all of the goals and objectives or until April 19, Adam's third birthday."

"Will we be working directly with you on any of these things?" Elena asked.

"Yes. You and I will need to meet once a week, either in your home or my office, to discuss any changes that need to be made, and I will assess Adam's progress monthly using the ELAP, the Early Learning Accomplishment Profile, which is the same measure we used before." Miguel took a breath. He hated the overwhelmed look in their eyes. He hated that he had to give them all this information, but he wanted them to know how committed he was to their son's success. "Please, take a moment to absorb all this, and then ask me any questions you might have."

Elena and Jon took a few quiet seconds just to breathe, each wondering whether this was only the beginning of a terribly long road.

"One more thing," Miguel broke the silence that had settled into the conversation. "Have you considered having him evaluated by a psychologist? He shows some signs of pervasive development disorder, and I think you would benefit from a formal evaluation. I've worked with Dr. Don Frazier before. He's great with small children. He could do an evaluation that would provide a diagnosis, and ultimately more help for Adam, should he need it." Miguel extended one of the psychologist's cards to Elena. Elena didn't know much about this disorder, but if this would help her son, then she would do it.

She looked down at the raised ink on the card and knew that she needed to give him a call.

CHAPTER 5
FIRST DIAGNOSIS

Three weeks later, Elena watched her husband shave over their bathroom sink. She noted the precision with which the blade hugged his strong jaw and remembered how she used to run her fingers from his ear to his collarbone. They'd met their junior year of high school, in a physics class. Elena had been enrolled by accident— she was supposed to be in physical education—but once she was assigned a lab partner and saw his green eyes shining over a letterman's jacket, she decided to stick with the class. Most people don't believe in love at first sight, but Elena knew it was possible. She only wished her life now was as perfect as it was in their prom pictures. On their wedding day, she'd snuck over to his apartment to watch him get ready. As he moved the razor over his cheeks, she'd joked that he was shaving off his single life. She wondered what he was shaving off now. Maybe the frustration that the past two-and-a-half years had brought or possibly all hope for a normal life for their little boy? She shook off that thought—*where had it come from?*—and went back to her flat iron.

"You okay, Laney?" Jon still used her high school nickname when he sensed something was wrong with her.

"Just thinking." She bit her lip, a nervous habit. "I just—I have wanted this evaluation for Adam for so long, but now that we're getting the results, I'm kind of a mess."

"I know, baby. But, if there's a problem, it's better to know now and start fixing it. Adam has to get it together by kindergarten. How else am I going to teach him to throw that baseball?" Now Jon was the one who looked wistful.

Jon had been an all-star pitcher in high school when he met Elena. On their wedding night, in a champagne stupor, he told her that he fantasized about a little boy with the same curly mop of black hair she'd had when he met her. He saw himself setting up a T in the yard and teaching him to swing a bat. His eyes began to itch with prickly tears, so he scratched his nose and reached for his allergy spray.

"Damn pollen in the air," he muttered. "I think the orange blossoms are in full effect." He wiped his face of the remaining shaving cream with a hot washcloth and disappeared into their walk-in closet to pick out his clothes for their meeting with Dr. Frazier.

• • •

Dr. Frazier liked the Phillips family, and although it was never easy to be the one who broke bad news to parents, it was more difficult when they were as stressed as this family. When it was time for their appointment—during which he would give them Adam's diagnosis—he was surprised that they walked into the office without their children. After ushering them to the two chairs across from his desk, he asked, "Where are the little people?"

Jon smiled. "My parents are watching them at our house. We promised them we wouldn't be more than an hour or two."

Dr. Frazier smiled back at Jon. "I'll keep this as brief as possible. Now, Mr. and Mrs. Phillips, as you know, we spent quite a bit of time with you and Adam. After looking at all the assessment information, we believe Adam meets the criteria for what is called a pervasive development disorder. More specifically, he meets the criteria for Pervasive Developmental Disorder, not otherwise specified, or PDD-NOS." Dr. Frazier paused, giving them time and space to process the information.

Elena's heart fell into her stomach, making her feel queasy. She took Jon's hand; he was sitting straight and rigid, looking almost as though he hadn't heard Dr. Frazier's words.

"I'm happy to answer any questions you have, but let me explain the diagnosis first. According to the Diagnostic and Statistical Manual of Mental Disorders, Fourth Edition, or DSM-IV," Dr. Frazier adjusted his paperwork so he could read the text to them, "this refers to a 'severe and pervasive impairment in the development of reciprocal social interaction or verbal and nonverbal communication skills, or when stereotyped behavior, interests, and activities are present, but the criteria are not met for a specific Pervasive Developmental Disorder or another disorder.' I'll translate that into English for you."

"Please," Jon said, with an edge to his voice.

"In DSM-IV, there are five forms of Pervasive Developmental Disorder. There is Autistic Disorder, Rett's Disorder, Childhood Disintegrative Disorder, Asperger's

Disorder, and Pervasive Developmental Disorder NOS. While Adam shows significant impairment in social interaction and communication, and a pattern of delays consistent with autistic disorder, he doesn't display restricted repetitive and stereotyped patterns of behavior, interests, and activities to a clinically significant degree at this time, that would be necessary for an autism diagnosis. His presentation appears to be associated with PDD-NOS. Some would say then that he is autistic-*like*. Our assessment of Adam indicates that he needs therapy and intervention to address developmental delays, social interaction, and communication skills."

Autistic-like. Autism was Elena's worst fear. It had been mentioned in so much of what she'd read about language disorders, but she purposely shoved the possibility aside. She didn't even want to think the word *autism*, and just that morning she'd said a prayer that it wouldn't be spoken today. Her boy who was born on Easter, crying so loudly that the whole floor of the hospital knew he'd arrived—he couldn't . . . he just couldn't.

"Well. That's good—right?" Jon sat back in his chair, and when he spoke again, he realized he was holding his breath. "I mean, we can get the therapy started now and by the time he's, what, five years old we can expect him to be normal for his age?"

Elena looked at Dr. Frazier, hopeful that he would confirm what her husband just said, but he just said, "Let's focus on today. I'll forward my evaluation and findings to your Birth to Three team so that our efforts are collaborative. Are there any other questions I can answer right now?"

The room was silent until Elena spoke, her voice little

more than a whisper. "I really don't know what to say. I think we need to digest this and ask you questions as they arise. Thank you so much, Dr. Frazier. We look forward to working with you."

Jon was quiet, his eyes scanning the papers before he abruptly stood and stuck out his hand for the psychologist to shake. "Thank you for everything. We'll see you soon."

In the car, Jon slammed his hand against the steering wheel. "Three words! Three words! That's what the last guy from the county said. Three words!"

"Well, it's a—"

"This guy quacks like a duck," Jon interrupted. "Adam can do anything that other kids can do. We just have to start pushing him. Hell, Shannon reads at four and a half. We should do those flashcards with him the way we did with her. He'll get there. We got this."

"No. No, we don't, Jon." Elena tried to keep her voice even and low to calm down her husband. "If we 'got this,' he wouldn't be here. I don't know what we could do to make this better without some help. We need to give this a try."

Jon was quiet, and Elena could feel the energy in the car return to normal.

After a few minutes of driving in silence, she said, "Remember when he was tiny and grunted all the time?" A faint smiled crossed Elena's lips at the memory.

"Carl . . ." Jon laughed, referencing their comparison of their son to Billy Bob Thorton in *Slingblade*. "I remember lying in the bed with you both, and while you'd nurse him, he'd go to town with the noises. It was so cute . . . only because I thought he would outgrow it. Now there's

a possibility we'll never be able to tease him about that."
Jon trailed off. "'Autistic-like,' Jesus."

Elena's heart jumped at the words. She was fighting
a deepening sense of panic beneath her calm exterior.

CHAPTER 6
CAN I GET A HIGH FIVE?

Elena looked down at the Discover card bill and sighed. She and Jon had always prided themselves on being a debt-free household. But when Adam's case was turned over to the school district on August 19, their insurance refused to cover the co-pays for the same therapists, and two years of $200 a week quickly caught up with their finances. But the therapies *helped*. Lyndsey was so much fun with Adam. One afternoon, she filled both their mouths with spaghetti and got him to make noises. This helped Adam focus on the space in his mouth and how he could form different sounds—it was a way to get him to babble and eventually speak. Bruce, meanwhile, mostly focused on sensory regulation and integration strategies with Adam. He would put him in a laundry basket and poke a feather duster through the holes in the side. Adam learned to anticipate where the tickle would come from next, and he loved that game; what he didn't know was that Bruce was helping him to also engage and interact with others. Now Adam could nonverbally indicate what he wanted, and he even spoke a few words. Elena thought back to his third birthday, when he walked her to the refrigerator and pointed. "Juice." She cried with relief that she was able to give her son something she knew he wanted.

The next day, Adam would be starting kindergarten. He'd done so well in the special education pre-kindergarten class that the school district wanted to try a half-day mainstream schedule. They maintained that the social interaction with typically developing peers would prove helpful in Adam's development. Elena knew the transition would be tough for Adam, and she braced herself for the change. Resigned, she put the Discover card bill back into the "To Be Paid" bin she kept on her desk and walked back into the living room, where Lyndsey was finishing a session with Adam.

"You did so well today! Can I get a high five?" Lyndsey was almost nose-to-nose with Adam, and she placed her hand over his and guided it to her free palm. Hand-over-hand teaching was huge. "You're a big boy, going to big boy school tomorrow. You're going to have so much fun with your teachers, right?"

"Fun," Adam repeated.

"Yes," Lyndsey looked adoringly at Adam. She'd been working with him for the better part of three years, and the Phillipses had become like family to her. Adam was such a neat little boy and had grown up to be so handsome. She remembered the little guy who had barely looked at her years ago and was amazed by the athletic build and buzz cut before her. "It's time for me to go now, Adam. I'll see you next week. Bye-bye." She waved at Adam and, his eyes flicking between Lyndsey and Elena, he raised a hand of his own.

"Hey," Elena said, walking with Lyndsey toward the

front door. "I was meaning to ask you about Dr. Stanley Greenspan. I keep coming across his name in my research. What do you know about his work?"

Lyndsey smiled and nodded. "He's a child psychiatrist who developed the Developmental, Individual Differences, Relationship-Based model, or DIR®. Floortime™[1] is a method and philosophy that is a major part of the DIR model; it's often used for developing social emotional skills in kids with autism. It's described in the book *Engaging Autism*, by Drs. Stanley Greenspan and Serena Wieder. I use part of DIR in my own practice of speech therapy. Things like 'creating a shared experience,' 'taking the child's lead,' and 'harnessing his natural interests.' It's all about improving developmental foundations by meeting kids where they're at—in other words, by engaging them at their level with activities they enjoy—in order to strengthen their social emotional skills over time. The *vrooming* of cars on the carpet that Adam and I do to warm up most days is an example of Floortime. That's how I try to engage him in therapy. I use his natural interests and then build upon his capacities in attention, regulation, engagement and relating, two-way communication, and problem solving. These are all areas that are usually achieved pretty early in typically developing kids, but they are delayed in kids with autism spectrum disorders."

Elena nodded, chewing her lower lip. "Can I do Floortime with him on my own?"

"Of course!" Lyndsey peered around the corner, and they both looked at Adam sitting on the carpet, lining

---

1 DIR® and Floortime™ are trademarks or registered trademarks of the Interdisciplinary Council on Developmental and Learning Disorders.

up his cars. "Just set aside twenty-minute blocks of time each day to follow Adam's lead and harness his natural interests to create a shared experience. It doesn't have to be on the floor, literally. You can do it anywhere. The time you spend in the pool with Adam is an excellent example. You're naturally using so many of Greenspan's techniques that I'd recommend looking into it further. *Engaging Autism* is a great book."

Elena nodded, reaching forward to embrace Lyndsey. "I'll do that. Thanks for everything, Lynds. The way you work with Adam, your suggestion of Birth to Three when we first met . . . I don't know that we'd be looking forward to tomorrow if it weren't for you."

Lyndsey smiled back at the woman who was not just one of her employers but now a close friend. "You and Adam did all the hard work. I'm so happy for all of us."

CHAPTER 7
THE PRINCIPAL'S OFFICE

The first day of kindergarten was emotional for Elena and Jon. She remembered her teary eyes when she dropped Shannon at Mrs. Baker's door two years earlier, and she couldn't believe that Adam had made it into the same classroom as his sister. She kissed her son and walked him to his desk. Since she knew she would be emotional, she'd taken the day off work. She and Jon drove back home, where Jon went back to bed and Elena cleaned up the kitchen from breakfast. She settled on the couch with a book and dozed off for a few minutes when her phone rang.

"Mrs. Phillips? This is Celina, Mr. Proctor's secretary."

Mr. Proctor was the principal at the elementary school, and although Elena had seen him at assemblies and parent meetings, she'd never spoken to him directly.

"Yes, ma'am. How can I help you?"

"Adam seems to be having trouble adjusting to his new class. Could you come down here?"

"Sure, I'll be right there." Elena grabbed her purse and flew out the door.

In Mr. Proctor's office, the principal was scowling as

Mrs. Baker held an ice pack to her eye, recounting Adam's behavior in the classroom. She had been moving the students from center to center in her kindergarten class. She played the same song that she had played for years, "Move it, move it, move it. The fun has just begun." Adam was engrossed in his painting project, and although it was Sally's time to move to the art station and Adam's turn to move to the kitchen, he made no move to undo his smock or stop the yellow streaks he was painting on the poster paper with broad strokes.

"Adam, it's time to move, sweetie. It's time to go play in the kitchen and give Sally a turn with the paint."

Adam acted as though he hadn't heard her. He continued gripping the light brown wood of the paintbrush between his fingers.

"Adam, if you don't move, you're going to have to go to the Quiet Thinking Chair," Mrs. Baker explained patiently. The rest of the students had moved on and were happily playing in their centers, except Sally, who was getting upset that she couldn't paint.

"I promised Daddy I'd paint him a pony," Sally said, sticking out her bottom lip. "But stupid Adam won't move."

Elena cringed, waiting for the turning point in Mrs. Baker's story.

"He still didn't want to stop painting," Mrs. Baker said, "so I guided him to what we call the 'quiet thinking chair.' It's where students go when they need a minute to calm down. He didn't like it, but he went. The next thing I knew, though, Adam had climbed the bookshelf behind the chair. When I went over to talk him down, he jumped and landed on me."

Elena shook her head, mortified at the bruise deepening beneath Mrs. Baker's eye. "I am so sorry, Mrs. Baker," she said. "He likes to climb things and doesn't do well with change."

Mrs. Baker tried to chuckle. "He's just a very rambunctious and active little boy—very different from your daughter."

"He is," Elena agreed. "How do we handle this?"

"He's doing fine in the classroom now," Mr. Proctor cut in. "We have a sub for Mrs. Baker. Let's leave him in and see what happens. Thank you so much for coming down, Mrs. Phillips."

CHAPTER 8
FAMILY FIRST

"Elena, you have a call on line three."

Elena closed her eyes for a moment and sighed. She knew exactly who was calling her at work; in fact, she got at least three of these summonses a week.

"This is Elena Phillips," she said into the phone, praying for the off chance that it was a vendor or the home office.

"Mrs. Phillips, this is Mr. Proctor." The school principal's voice droned in her ear. He was obviously as tired of making the phone calls to Elena as she was to receiving them.

"Yes, sir. What's going on today?"

"As you know, Adam always seems to have trouble when it's time to finish story circle and start art, but today he actually scratched another student's face hard enough to break her skin. He then retaliated against Mrs. Baker when she tried to pull him off by biting her arm again. When she released him, he hit his head on the desk, hard. The school nurse has evaluated all of them, and we're treating his head with ice. The other parents are here, and we need you to come pick Adam up. He can't finish the day here."

Elena sighed, holding back her tears. "I understand. I have to call my district manager to get someone to cover the store for the rest of my shift, but I'll be there as soon as I can."

She hung up the phone and paused for a moment before she dialed Alicia's cell phone number. It was the second time this week she'd needed someone to cover her shift so she could get Adam home from school early. She knew this was reflecting poorly on her performance, but what else could she do? *Family first* was what she always told her co-managers and associates. The store could run without them temporarily, but they were essential to their families. Since she'd trained Alicia, she was sure this would pass and everything would be fine again once Adam adjusted to his new class—which actually wasn't so new anymore. It was March. Kindergarten was almost over.

Elena shifted her car into gear and drove the few minutes to the school. As she paused at the Stop sign on the corner, the reality of her situation hit her. Last week she'd gone to get Adam because he'd smeared his feces all over the boys' bathroom wall. While he was completely toilet trained—he had been since he was four—he had taken to acting out in the bathroom. She was mortified as she cleaned her son with rough, brown paper towels wetted in a sink that barely touched her thigh. Thankfully, she had a beach towel in her backseat that she wrapped him in as she left the school. That didn't stop an older class from staring at them as she walked him to their car. "Is he going swimming? No fair. I wish she was my mom." What killed her as she heard those kids' hushed remarks was her thought: *And I wish I were your mom, too.* Her love and devotion to her son was everlasting, but at that moment, she'd love to have been visiting campus for an art show or Mother's Day brunch. Anything but why she was there. She felt ashamed for . . . everything.

She sighed and pulled into the circular drive in front of the elementary school's main office. The disinfectant-heavy air invaded her nostrils as soon as she opened the door. Celina, who was out front, motioned to Mr. Proctor's door without even looking up. Such had become the routine.

Mr. Proctor shifted uncomfortably in his seat as he addressed Elena, seated next to her son in a scratchy black chair in the principal's white-walled office. "Mrs. Phillips, we need to have a conference about Adam's behavior. Now isn't the time, obviously, but can we schedule a time where both you and your husband are available?"

"I'd like that very much, Mr. Proctor. In fact," Elena took a deep breath, "it's obvious to me that this mainstream classroom isn't working for Adam. I'd like to schedule a meeting to review the Individualized Education Plan, his progress, and also talk about some changes." Elena winced as she said it, feeling both demanding of Mr. Proctor and as though she were somehow giving up on the idea of Adam's "normalcy." But she'd read that the district was legally required to schedule an IEP meeting at her request, and she knew it was in Adam's best interests.

"At the IEP meeting, we can all work together on a solid plan that will allow Adam to benefit from his education," Elena continued. "His speech therapist and occupational therapist have been working with Adam since he was two; they'll have great recommendations for your teachers." Elena shifted, noticing that Adam was getting restless. He'd stood and was stepping from one foot to another, a clear sign that he was agitated and possibly about to melt down all over again. She pulled her son into her lap and wrapped her arms around his torso as tightly as she could. She felt his heartbeat slow through his back.

"All right, Mrs. Phillips," Mr. Proctor said. "We can schedule the IEP meeting within the next three weeks. This will give our school team some time to review records and complete some observations of Adam. Then we can all get together and discuss the findings."

"Thank you, Mr. Proctor," Elena put Adam on the floor and held his hand to guide him to their car. She would change them both into their swimsuits as soon as they got home. The pool would keep Adam from acting out for at least an hour and would hopefully wear him out enough so that he would watch an episode of *Barney* while she prepared dinner for the family.

The afternoon went more smoothly than Elena had hoped. She ran her fingers over her son's slippery skin as he glided past her toward the deep end of the pool. She saw his head come up for breath, and he continued, touching the back wall, pulling himself out of the water and diving in again. He swam right back to his mother, wrapping his legs around her waist and floating his head back. She reached up to his ribs and gave him a tickle. He laughed, sitting up so that she was holding him. He wrapped his arms around her neck now, and she was holding him, looking down at his perfectly shaped ears and his shoulders that were becoming more muscular every day. He giggled into her collarbone as she poked at his armpits, and for a moment, she knew her son, intimately, the way she should.

After cuddling on the couch and both taking a nap, Elena found herself a little pink cheeked from the sun but smiled with the pleasure of the afternoon. With the *Barney* theme music drifting in from the family room, she turned around and devoted her full attention to chopping carrots for the stew she was making. Then, right behind her: *Bam!* She jumped and whirled around to see Adam sitting on his knees on the hard tile right behind her.

"Adam!" Elena cried.

Adam stood but didn't respond. He looked focused and purposeful, not at all hurt by the impact of his knees on the tile, despite the fact that circular red marks were already blooming on his skin. Without making a sound, he pulled himself onto the kitchen island and, before Elena had a chance to respond, jumped to his knees again. The sickening sound of bone on floor made Elena gasp.

"Adam!" she cried sharply. "Stop!"

No sooner had those words come out of her mouth than Adam started screaming. He banged his head against the tile, slapping the floor with his palms. Elena bent down and scooped him into her arms. "It's okay, sweetie. It's okay. Mommy didn't mean to talk so loud. Mommy is sorry." After another sob, Adam started to compose himself and maneuvered off her lap and back to the living room. Elena stayed on the floor, shaken. He could have broken his knees. Or hit his head in the fall. And banging his forehead straight into the ground? What if she hadn't been here to stop him? The *what-ifs* crowded her mind, filling her with fear for the future. She led him back into the living room where she sat on the couch long enough to ensure he was once again engrossed in *Barney* before she went back into the kitchen.

She had started dinner again when the front door opened. "Adam?" she called. Panic that he had let himself out of the house rose into her throat. "Adam!"

"It's me, Mom," she heard Shannon's voice echo from the foyer. "Marissa's mom gave me a ride home."

Oh, my God. I forgot to pick up Shannon after her piano lesson. Elena was mortified. "Shannon! I—I'm so sorry." She rushed into the living room to hug her daughter. The second grader stood in front of her mother and gave her a smile. Her two front teeth had fallen out early and were already replaced with adult teeth, leaving the rest of her mouth looking tiny by comparison.

"It's okay. Listen." Shannon's green eyes were gleaming. She bounced on the balls of her feet. "I have *huge* news."

"I'm all ears, sweetheart," Elena said. She put an arm around Shannon, guiding her daughter into the kitchen. "Here, sit down, and tell me while I cook dinner."

Shannon took a deep, preparatory breath. Excitement radiated from her small frame. "So, I won the class spelling bee today, which means that I'm going to compete for the second grade title! We're having it after school next Thursday, and we're supposed to invite our families. Only one person from each class is able to participate and it's *me!*" Shannon beamed at her accomplishment.

"Darling, I'm so proud of you!" Elena gushed, reaching down to hug Shannon. "Thursday is when Adam has speech therapy with Miss Lyndsey, so I need to be here, but Daddy will be happy to go cheer you on for the whole family."

Shannon's face fell for just a moment before she pulled herself together. "It's okay, Mom. Maybe he can video it so that we can all watch it together that night."

"That would be perfect, sweetie," Elena said, swallowing past the tinge of guilt. "Do you want to help me with dinner?"

"I'd like to get my homework done first. I'll be done in time to eat." Shannon scampered down the hallway and closed her bedroom door before Elena could see the tears running down her cheeks.

CHAPTER 9
HANG IN THERE

"Adam has been participating in a more inclusive special education arrangement at school," said Dr. Kemper, the school psychologist who had performed part of the first special education evaluation for Adam. A full beard grew across his face, and he had a no-nonsense attitude but kind eyes behind wire-rimmed glasses. "We all talked at the school level, and based upon our observations of your son, we think Adam would do much better in a smaller and self-contained classroom setting."

Elena relaxed as much as she could into the hard black chair. Her eyes scanned the posters on the wall and landed on the one that she found particularly obnoxious. "Hang in there," it read in white letters as a cat's claws connected a scared feline to a tree branch. She knew the feeling, suspended with little more than dead skin keeping her in the tree, but the poster made her gag and not smile. Still, despite the cheesy posters and the uncomfortable chair, the rough blue carpet and the metal desk that clanged every time the school psychologist crossed and uncrossed his legs—she was relieved. No more having to call into work. Maybe Adam could thrive here. "That sounds ideal, Dr. Kemper."

"We've made arrangements for him to start in the new room on Monday. There might be an initial period of adjustment for Adam, but I think he will gel there nicely. Now, we've also changed Adam's Individualized Education Plan." He handed Elena and Jon the preprinted forms.

Jon looked over the paperwork. "I thought we could have more input. We are his parents, after all."

"Well, yes."

"My wife and I have discussed the IEP with Adam's speech and occupational therapists, and we wanted to incorporate some of the techniques we're using at home."

"Such as?" Dr. Kemper asked with interest.

"Well," Jon started, "recently, Bruce, our OT, started sponge therapy with Adam. It's a little strange sounding, but whenever Adam makes a bad choice—like hitting, kicking, or biting—we dump wet sponges out of a bucket. We say 'pick up, pick up, pick up' and he does. Then we repeat 'no kicking, no kicking!' If he repeats the behavior, we dump the sponges again. It's working wonders at home, but we've found it is very important to be consistent with the method all the time and across all people working with him."

"Well, Mr. Phillips, I'm glad that you're finding good strategies for Adam at home," Dr. Kemper said. "But you'll find that our special education staff also have a very effective way of doing things."

"Yes, but, in order for therapies to be effective, don't we need consistency?" Elena broke in. "What about what's best for *Adam*?"

"Of course, we have Adam's best interests at heart," said Dr. Kemper. "Our goal is to get the behavioral problems under control so that we can return him to a more inclusive classroom model. His education is our first priority." Dr. Kemper nodded toward the IEP paperwork. "You'll see that we've made provisions so that he can wear the hoodie he is so attached to while he is indoors."

A tiny olive branch, Elena thought. She was skeptical but felt like her hands were tied. "We'll give it a shot. What about the other kids in his class?"

"We have a variety of kids in there, with a range of disabilities. However, we have a four-to-one student-to-teacher ratio and are seeing some real success."

CHAPTER 10
SCALING BACK

A month later, Elena was working with Alicia—now her district manager—when she got a phone call.

"Mrs. Phillips, it's Mr. Proctor."

The familiar dread built up in Elena's stomach.

"Adam is being aggressive again. Today, he pushed a less physically capable child out of his wheelchair. The other child became emotional, and Adam proceeded to stab him with a pencil. The other child is at the emergency room—we think he needs his hand stitched. Mrs. Phillips, Adam needs to go home this afternoon."

"I understand. I'll be there as quickly as possible." Elena hung up the phone and looked up at Alicia.

"Again?" Alicia asked.

"Yep. I'm glad you're here today. Could you close the store?"

"I can, but look—could Jon maybe get him today? We need to review our projections for next quarter."

He stabbed a kid in a wheelchair! Elena thought. But she read the seriousness in Alicia's eyes. "He's sleeping, but I'll see if he wakes up for the phone."

Jon did wake up and grumpily agreed to pick up Adam

from school. Elena was relieved, not only that she didn't have to miss work but also that she didn't have to spend the afternoon with her son. She felt guilty that the thought even crossed her mind.

"Our ADS is getting close to seventy-five . . . Elena, are you with me?" Alicia's voice startled Elena, who was ashamed that she'd been lost in thought.

Elena looked Alicia right in the eye. "Sure."

Alicia looked at her. "I remember when you were pregnant with Adam. You and Jon were so excited to have a little boy. You guys joked that you were living the American dream with your boxed set."

Elena smiled, but she could feel that something was coming.

"Listen, I respect everything that you do," Alicia said. "You trained me, and I owe my career to you in a lot of ways. But, Elena, your family needs you more than we do."

Without warning, Elena burst into tears. "Everyone needs more than I can give right now."

Alicia put her arm around her colleague. "What if you scaled back to part time? Just temporarily. When you get things figured out with Adam, your job will be waiting for you again. I promise."

"Really?" Elena sniffled. "I didn't think this was an option, but—yes, okay. That's very kind. I'll just have to talk it over with Jon."

Alicia sighed. "I need you to take this offer, now. Corporate isn't happy with your absences, and this was my solution to keep you on. You have twelve weeks' unpaid FMLA, but I'd rather keep you on the payroll."

Elena wiped her eyes. She was stunned. *She'd almost*

lost her job? While she knew things weren't perfect, she never imagined they would come to this.

"Okay," Elena managed, her voice strangled. "I accept."

"Good. Now, let's work out these projections so that we can cut your hours starting next week."

That night, Elena turned the key in the lock expecting a quiet house. It was nine p.m., both of the kids should be in bed, and Jon would be getting ready for work. She went into the living room to tell him everything that had happened at work, but he started in as soon as he saw her.

"Adam totally freaked out in the car," Jon said, roughly drying his hair with a towel. "He was banging his head against the window as we sat in the carpool lane waiting for Shannon to get out of school. I'm exhausted! And I still have a full day of work ahead of me."

"They almost fired me." Elena's voice was small.

"What?"

"Alicia said corporate wasn't happy with my absences and that I needed to step down to part time, or I was gone, basically. So, yeah." Elena sat down on the edge of the bed, shoulders slumped. "I don't anticipate you having any more sleepless days."

"How are we going to keep up with our bills? We're already behind from years of this!" Jon's voice was rising, and he stood with anger in his eyes. "Elena, what were you thinking? How did this happen?"

"Is that what's most important to you? Money? Our son is practically drowning . . . *I'm* drowning! We have to get some control over at least one aspect of our lives, and I don't like it, either, but this is the best solution. Your afternoon? That's my every day."

The truth of Elena's last statement hit Jon between the

eyes, and his stance softened as he sat next to his wife. "Okay. Jeff needs a part-time mechanic to work mornings. If you're home more, I can pick up shifts there. We'll make it work."

After a moment, Elena softened in his arms. "We always have," she whispered.

CHAPTER 11
REEVALUATION

"Hurry, hurry guys," Elena called out to her children, who were still dawdling with their cereal in the breakfast nook. While Adam only ate spaghetti and fried chicken when he was home alone with Elena, he would thankfully at least try some foods that Shannon was eating. "We have five minutes to get out the door!"

She heard laughter coming from the kitchen and walked in to make sure the kids knew she wasn't fooling around. Shannon was making faces at Adam over their bowls, and he was laughing hysterically.

"What's going on?" Elena asked, a smile playing at her lips.

"Adam farted at the table! I was trying to explain how rude that is, but he got stuck on my 'stink face.' We haven't moved on yet." Shannon giggled.

Elena playfully rolled her eyes. "Where are your shoes, Adam? I have to get to work!"

She grabbed backpacks as Shannon helped Adam get his shoes on. He was in a great mood this morning, which was usually the case when Shannon was there. He and his sister had connected especially well over the past year, and with Adam entering second grade, Elena hoped they would continue to bond as he got older. In the afternoons, however, Adam was a different person. Both Adam and Elena were bruised and busted from his outbursts, which included everything from flailing on the floor to punching at windows. Elena had gone through the house and "Adam-proofed" it, putting the family's most valuable things in her walk-in closet. But that didn't stop him from somehow finding and destroying anything fragile or expensive. She still felt a wave of sadness when she thought about her and Jon's wedding china, which was smashed against the dining room table by Adam's hands. She'd taken him to the emergency room for stitches, crying as she watched the doctor pulling shards of powder blue plate from her son's hands with tweezers. He was growing bigger every day and becoming harder for Elena, who was only five-three and a size four, to manage.

Plus, she still wasn't seeing the results she would have liked at school. The calls to come pick him up only came every other week, but as a result, she was still part time at the store a year later. Jon was working two jobs but finding success as a mechanic at his friend's shop in the morning. He had built the reputation of the shop to higher quality with his knowledge of German luxury cars, but that didn't stop the black rings around his eyes. He worked his usual eleven p.m. to seven a.m. shift at UPS, then went to Denny's for a Grand Slam and a pot of coffee before heading to the shop from eight to noon. He slept as much as he could in the afternoons, but when Adam was home with Elena—without Shannon to distract him with piano or silly faces—that wasn't much.

Adam thrashed and bucked, screaming at seemingly insignificant changes or choices. Elena pulled him into her lap to hold him when she could, but she often needed Jon to get up and help her restrain him.

Elena clocked out of work at noon and got in her car. When she arrived home, she slid into her yoga pants and turned on the TV. The opening credits to *Jersey Shore* filled her living room as she headed to her refrigerator for the half-empty bottle of sauvignon blanc. This afternoon, Shannon had piano lessons, which meant that the three o'clock bus would only bring Adam home. She sighed and slunk onto her couch with her glass of wine, a new tradition on days the school didn't call her to pick up her son early.

Upon finishing the bottle of wine, her phone rang. *Shit, I hope it's not the school. I can't drive right now!* But the caller ID said Lyndsey, and her shoulders immediately loosened.

"I found someone you need to see."

"Is he handsome?" Elena joked.

"Well, yes," Lyndsey laughed, "but that's not why you need to see him. He's a psychologist I'm working with on another of my cases. He's a super nice guy who specializes in PDD and autism spectrum disorders. Another of my clients—he's older than Adam is but shares some of the same issues—his family worked with Dr. Mohr, got an official diagnosis of autism, and BAM! He's in a classroom specializing in Autism Spectrum Disorder, and I'm seeing a lot of success with him. I know that PDD-NOS is on the spectrum, but, as someone who cares for your family, I have to tell you, it's time for Adam to be reevaluated. I have his number, do you want it?"

Elena was taken aback. Lyndsey had a tendency to talk fast and was so passionate about her work that she could get excited when she found a breakthrough for one of her families, but the A-word? Again? After all, her son just had something that was "like" autism, she was told. Even then, Elena didn't want to think about it in those terms. She wanted to hear "Pomp and Circumstance" at his high school graduation, to dance with him at his wedding—all the things that every mother envisioned for her son. While those dreams were becoming less tangible, even in her wildest imagination, she did at least want to see some semblance of normalcy for Adam's adult life. She couldn't take care of him forever, the old lady chasing down her grown son in the grocery store. Obviously, though, school wasn't working well for Adam, and drinking in the afternoon wasn't a good sign of things to come for her, either.

"Let me get his number. I'll talk it over with Jon when he gets home."

Lyndsey gave her more information, and when Elena hung up the phone, the alarm chime indicated that Jon opened the front door.

"How's it going?" His sleepy eyes smiled at his wife, until he saw the wine bottle and empty glass next to it on the kitchen counter. "Really? Elena, it's barely one."

"I know. I'm sorry. It was . . ."

"Laney." Jon's face settled, and Elena could see the deepening lines between his heavy eyes. His face was scratchy and unshaven, and he was starting to look a lot older than his thirty-three years. Without a word, they had a conversation, and shame flushed Elena's cheeks.

"I know." Elena looked down.

Jon put his arm around his wife as he sat on the couch. "What can I do?"

Tears ran down her cheeks as she looked into the green eyes that had pulled her in almost twenty years ago. "I just got off the phone with Lyndsey. She thinks we need to have Adam reevaluated for autism."

"What? Why?"

"She said that while the PDD diagnosis has been helpful for us and is a good place to start, if Adam has autistic disorder, she knows a psychiatrist who specializes in this area. Adam has changed a bit over the years, too, and it wouldn't hurt to have another evaluation. I think it might help. She's going to email a few things to me, including a brief survey. I think we should do it. She's seen success with other clients once they have a formal diagnosis of autism."

Jon looked down. "Well, I guess we have to do *something*. Because what we're doing right now ain't working."

CHAPTER 12
AUTISTIC DISORDER

Elena and Jon went armed with an arsenal of information to Dr. Mohr's office. He was younger than Elena had expected, and Lyndsey was right—he was also attractive. His dark hair waved on his head, offsetting his dark complexion. He smiled, and his full lips parted to show two rows of perfectly straight, white teeth. He extended a hand to the Phillipses before stooping down to Adam's level.

"Hi, buddy. We're going to have some fun today, but first I need to talk to your mom and dad. Here are some cars to play with." He produced two Hot Wheels from his pocket and handed them to Adam, who took them and banged them together.

"Please, have a seat," he motioned to the two empty chairs in front of his desk. "Elena, I'm going to start with you. I need you to think back and tell me all about your pregnancy."

Elena sighed. "Okay . . ."

"Now, during the pregnancy, did you use drugs, tobacco, or alcohol?"

"No," Elena said defensively. "I mean, I had a few glasses of wine before I knew I was pregnant, but nothing major. I stopped when the test read positive."

Dr. Mohr continued, pressing Elena for details about Adam's birth and whether or not she had breastfed him, and then moved to Jon for his recollection of events. So far, everything was typical. Her pregnancy was textbook, and Adam's time as a newborn was exhausting but not abnormally so.

"When did you first notice that something was different about Adam?" Dr. Mohr leaned in.

"His first birthday party," Elena said instantly. "He didn't want anyone near him except me. He wanted to play in the pool the whole time."

Jon took over, telling the doctor about their struggles over the past six years, describing the details of the tantrums, the lack of eye contact, the expressive and receptive language problems. While he was talking, Elena looked over at her son, still engrossed in the two cars Dr. Mohr had handed him the better part of an hour ago. His long, dark eyelashes fluttered as he banged the cars on top of each other. When he was a newborn, she'd looked at those lashes and wondered about the lucky woman who was going to fall in love with them.

"Your son is seven years old. I have to ask, why am I just seeing you now?" Dr. Mohr asked when Jon finished.

"As you'll be able to see from his medical records," Elena said, somewhat defensively, "we went with Birth to Three services first and then obtained the PDD-NOS diagnosis. The public school special education classroom strategies aren't working for Adam so far. We've talked to other families who have worked with you. You have a great reputation, so it made sense to . . ."

"I know," Dr. Mohr said, more gently, "and I'll do what I

can to help. I'm going to meet with Adam for a few hours and have our speech and occupational therapists work with him as well. You're welcome to wait in the lobby or go grab a bite to eat. We'll see you in a little while." He smiled as he ushered them out the door.

Elena couldn't possibly eat right now. She and Jon silently sat in the lobby, both flipping through magazines and absently watching the television that was playing Yo Gabba Gabba!

"What if he throws a big fit in there?" Jon looked over at his wife. "He could, especially with all those new people."

"They know what they're doing. He'll be fine," Elena replied, more to hear the words herself than to reassure her husband. "I couldn't eat, but a Diet Cherry Coke would be divine."

"Let's go to Sonic." Jon smiled. It used to be their place.

Elena laughed and took her husband's arm as he brought her back to the site of their first date.

Two hours later, Dr. Mohr sent a nurse out for Elena and Jon. Hand in hand, they walked back toward the office.

Adam was happily stacking books when Elena and Jon walked in. Dr. Mohr was behind his desk and stood to greet them. Elena ruffled Adam's hair as she walked by, and he shrugged.

"Was he okay?" she asked the doctor. "He didn't give you any problems, did he?"

"Oh, he was fine," Dr. Mohr smiled. "I do, however, have something to share with you. Would you please sit down?"

Elena's stomach tied up in knots and she grasped her husband's hand tighter as they walked over to the seats.

"Mr. and Mrs. Phillips, we spent quite a bit of time with

Adam today, and first, I have to say, he is a very nice boy."

"Thanks," said Elena. She smiled, but her stomach was trembling with trepidation at what the doctor would tell her next.

"Now, I'll go over the results of the assessment." Dr. Mohr paused, motioning to the chart he had spread across his desk. "We found Adam to be mostly nonverbal, his stereotyped behavior scored especially high, and he was particularly low with social interaction, completely ignoring me as I tried to engage him in play and other activities. His language, communication, and social interaction skills are very low relative to kids his age, and he demonstrates a number of sensory-based sensitivities. Overall, I would say that his presentation and the results are consistent with a diagnosis of autistic disorder."

For a moment, Elena couldn't breathe. While PDD-NOS was on the autism spectrum, it didn't carry with it the weight of classic autistic disorder. She felt paralyzed with loss as she leaned over into her husband, who wrapped his arms around her. She broke into tears against Jon's chest for all the things she wanted for her son—the things every parent dreams of for their child—that might not ever be. Crying also came as a relief. She finally had an answer to the question of what was wrong with her son. Soon she would have some documentation, some paperwork that would explain everything about Adam to the world. Maybe now he could finally get the help he needed at school. She looked up at her husband, whose cheeks were wet, too, and then over at the innocent, young, beautiful soul stacking books. He didn't deserve this. They didn't deserve this. But as a family—by God, they were not going to let autism defeat them.

PART II

CHAPTER 13
MEDICATION

"We're certainly going to miss him," Jennifer's eyes were wet with tears as she slid her arms around Adam's neck. He was seated at his desk, his mouth blue from the cupcakes that Elena brought in for him and Jennifer to share. He was at the end of fifth grade, and for the past two years, Jennifer had been his one-on-one aide. The school district worked it out so that she could go to middle school with him next year, but plans changed at the end of the year when Jon was offered a supervisory position with UPS in Madison, Wisconsin. The money was too good to pass up, good enough that Elena could give up her part-time job, and Jon wouldn't have to maintain a second job anymore. The worst part was pulling Adam away from Lyndsey and Bruce, who'd worked with him for almost ten years, and away from Jennifer and a school situation that was finally working for him.

Elena thought back to when they had received the autistic disorder diagnosis that explained so much about her son. On one level, they were not at all surprised, but on another, they had been truly stunned. She and Jon came home and cried together on and off for a day. She got in touch with Mr. Proctor the next morning and arranged a conference with him, Dr. Kemper, Dr. Mohr, and Ms. Pressnall, the special education director at the school. With the diagnosis and another IEP meeting, she was able to get Adam into a self-contained district classroom and program for children with autism. Despite everyone's best efforts, Adam still did not do very well at school. His meltdowns seemed to increase in frequency, duration, and length, and—most disturbingly—in violence. When he punched and knocked down his large male teacher just because he was working with someone else, the school finally gave in to Elena's argument that Adam needed a one-on-one aide. The school hired Jennifer Clark, a paraprofessional with an associate's degree in early childhood educational disorders. She was working on her bachelor's degree online, and the work with Adam proved perfect for her.

Recognizing that Elena was the "Adam expert," Jennifer scheduled weekly meetings with Elena and incorporated her thoughts and strategies into Adam's daily school life. She met with both Lyndsey and Bruce to incorporate the sponge therapy into their daily routine and got permission to let Adam have an hour on the swing sets each day, weather permitting. As the pool was at home, the swings seemed to be Adam's refuge at school. He spent that time rocking back and forth, propelling himself higher and higher. The sensory stimulation allowed him to better self-regulate; in turn, he was much calmer in the afternoons, more ready, willing, and available to do the academic schoolwork that the district expected of him. Jennifer provided Elena with the same sense of hope and purpose that Lyndsey had given her years ago. Both of these women loved her boy almost as much as she did, and she was thankful that they were in his life. Uprooting Adam from people with whom he had formed connections terrified Elena, but she looked forward to being able to devote more time and attention to him. Shannon, meanwhile, had continued to do well in school. She made friends easily and was excited about the move, as there was a quality performing arts high school in Madison. In addition to her 4.0 grade point average, she was becoming quite the concert pianist.

The summer stretched before Elena, and although she had two months until the moving company took their life to the bigger house awaiting them in Wisconsin's rolling hills, she was terrified at the prospect of finding the same resources for her son that she'd taken years to find in Florida. Each night, her laptop burned hot on her legs from her Google searches. She scoured sites for parents of children with autism, searched reviews of psychiatrists and programs, and tried to judge which would be the best for her son. She reached out to county services, and received a call back from Lauren Jefferies, a county caseworker liaison for the school district's special education program. Lauren listened to Elena's suggestions and noted the psychiatrists she recommended as having expertise in autism spectrum disorders before working to get the Phillips family settled into their new lives with the school district.

A few weeks later, when all the boxes were unpacked, Elena took Adam to meet Dr. Loretta Valentino, his new psychiatrist. Dr. Valentino had been working with children on the autism spectrum for the better part of her thirty-year career. She had reviewed his medical history, as well as psychological and educational evaluations, prior to meeting with Elena and Jon.

Dr. Valentino's office was covered in dark wood paneling and smelled faintly of sandalwood. Adam was excited to see that she had a set of DUPLO blocks and even removed his iPod earbuds in order to connect the blocks on the floor. Elena and Jon settled in on the dark brown leather couch as Dr. Valentino asked them how they were adjusting to the cooler Wisconsin weather. The doctor listened with her whole body, nodding and leaning forward, and the Phillipses immediately felt comforted in her presence.

"I've read a great deal about Adam's history, but I'd like for you to tell me more about who he is as a child and person," Dr. Valentino smiled warmly.

"I—of course," Elena was a little taken aback by the question. No one except those who'd worked closely with Adam had ever asked her about who he was as a person, including his strengths. It was a question that she and Shannon talked about often, laughing that Adam had become so good-looking and athletic that he would be a popular jock if he didn't have autism. She laughed with the doctor, and then the conversation took a more serious tone.

"I noticed in the records that Adam is not taking any medication," Dr. Valentino said. "Can you tell me the reason for that?"

"We've been working with behavioral therapies," Jon explained. "But we're certainly not opposed to medication at this point."

"We are open to whatever works," Elena reiterated, somewhat insincerely, as she and Jon were, in fact, opposed to the use of medication except as a last resort.

"Tell me about the times he gets very upset—the meltdowns. Have you had any success with the behavioral strategies?" Dr. Valentino asked.

"We have several meltdowns a day. Maybe three on average. Some days it feels as though that's all we have." Elena tried to make a joke, but the crack in her voice betrayed her pain. "They vary, though. Sometimes it's just a yell that goes on for fifteen minutes. Other times he is violent. Those are becoming more frequent. We had problems at his last school. He managed to fling part of a cinderblock at one of his classmates during recess." Elena shuddered at the memory. "It was awful."

Dr. Valentino nodded sympathetically. "He's ten, correct?"

Elena nodded.

"Puberty is coming. That can be a tough time even for typically developing kids—and their parents—but with Adam's aggression, an increase in size and strength will make him more difficult to control." She leaned forward in her chair. "I've had a great deal of success with a medication called Abilify, and I'd like to give it a try with Adam."

Elena still did not like the idea of medicating her son, but the doctor had addressed her greatest fear—that he would not get better. Everyone associated autism with young children, but the reality was that Adam wasn't getting better—he was only getting older. She looked over at Jon with trepidation, only to find that he was looking at her with determination. "Why don't we try it?" he asked her. "We can always take him off if it isn't working, right, doctor?"

"Of course." Dr. Valentino smiled. "I do think it's worth a try."

Elena took the prescription with shaky hands. She'd researched medication—parents on message boards talked about the change in their children when given pills to help with their temper or behavioral issues. Most of them talked about an increase in stereotypical behavior—facial tics, flapping of hands—but some had more serious consequences. Children were increasingly violent or self-injurious. She'd even read one case about a child who'd attempted to take his own life while on a medication. She spoke up, her voice unsteady. "What kinds of side effects can we expect?"

"A calmer Adam is our anticipated outcome," Dr. Valentino said reassuringly. "But you might see some sleeplessness, maybe a little weight gain. I know you're concerned, but we're going to monitor him closely."

CHAPTER 14
RESTLESS

Six weeks later, Adam's body twitched and jerked in Elena's arms. Her son, who was once so small, now came up to her shoulders, and she only had him by twenty pounds on the scale. He'd hit a growth spurt right after moving to Wisconsin, and the Abilify caused him to gain close to thirty-five pounds. Jon and Elena were going on close to thirty hours without sleep, and Elena's eyes ached at the thought of another sleepless night. He thrashed and bucked, grunting in frustration. She pulled his head to hers, pressing her face against his damp hair, and made the same shushing noise into his ear that she had when he was a baby. "Shhhhhh . . ." It wasn't rude; it was soothing, like white noise. "Adam has to go to school in the morning," she whispered to her child, "so he needs to get some sleep."

"No!" Adam cried.

While the move had been the best choice for the rest of the family, it couldn't have been worse for Adam. His new school had a special education department with more experience with autism spectrum disorders, but it was an unfamiliar environment and a huge change for Adam; as a result, his meltdowns had reached dramatic proportions. The Abilify made him restless, which meant he couldn't sit through a lesson. Just last week, when the teacher tried to redirect him, he threw himself onto the floor, wailing and banging his head and hands on the cold tile. Ms. White, his teacher, and her aide, Ralph, had to restrain him with his hands behind his back. He bucked back and head butted the teacher's aide, giving him two black eyes. The profuse vomiting that followed Adam's tantrum made Elena take him to the emergency room. The doctor couldn't be sure if it was the medication or a potential concussion that caused Adam's sickness, but his best guess was the medication since Adam's eyes weren't dilated and he showed no other symptoms of a concussion.

Elena called Dr. Valentino the morning after her trip to the emergency room and explained everything in detail. Dr. Valentino said that it wasn't uncommon for children with autism to have digestive issues and that he probably worked himself up with his tantrum to a point where he got sick to his stomach.

"But he's never had this before," Elena said, perplexed.

"There's a first time for everything, Elena. Try to get him to eat little bits at a time so his stomach isn't too full. Just imagine where his tantrum level would be if he weren't on the Abilify."

Dr. Valentino made a great point, Elena thought. If it was this bad now, what would he be like unmedicated? So she continued to give him his morning dose of the pills.

Elena had ensured that their house had all of Adam's favorite things—a swing set and a heated swimming pool—but as the temperatures fell, so did the number of hours he could spend with those activities. He grew frustrated having to stay inside all the time, so Elena and Jon bought him an iPad on which he could watch episodes of *Barney* and play minefield. He giggled when the grid exploded, and that smile was worth the extra three-hundred dollars they'd put on the credit card that weekend. Elena was grateful to get some sleep while Adam was at school but was miserable the rest of the time. She longed for the days when she would be able to go to work again, to have friends, but secretly feared those days would never come.

The next morning, after both getting about five hours of sleep, Elena took Adam to school. Ms. White was fitted with her acoustic guitar and smiled when they entered the room. "Adam, your friends are so glad you joined us," she exclaimed cheerfully. "Today we will play some music. It will be so much fun!"

Adam regarded the tall teacher skeptically, but Elena, desperate to get some sleep, kissed her son on his head and walked out of the classroom.

Elena managed to nap for almost an hour before her cell phone woke her up. "Hello?" she murmured into the phone.

"Mrs. Phillips, this is Mrs. Mathes, the principal at Adam's school. We've had an incident that requires your immediate attention. Please come as soon as you can."

Elena sat up in her bed, that familiar dread setting heavily in her stomach. She dressed quickly, pulling a brush through the knots on top of her head. Gone was the pulled-together appearance that she used to be able to fake, at least. She looked at herself as she brushed her teeth. She was wearing yoga pants and a t-shirt that Jon got for donating blood a few years ago. Her dark hair was pulled into an impromptu bun, accentuating the grey patches just above her ears. Her tired eyes sat back in her skull, and she noticed crow's feet extending from the corners.

At Adam's school, Elena shifted in her seat as the principal talked about Adam's day. The concrete block room was painted white but was mostly covered with bookcases displaying "Science Teacher of the Year" awards from the late 1980s and plaques with such platitudes as "A teacher takes a hand, opens a mind, and touches a heart." A fern growing in a corner looked in need of watering. Next to her, Adam tapped his foot, obviously still frustrated. The pat of his green Converse shoes on the carpet was maddening, so Elena put her hand on her son's leg, grabbing a handful of denim. His knee took up all the space in her palm, and she thought about not being able to grasp his kneecap someday the way she could now. His dark hair was unruly; as it was difficult to get him to sit still for a haircut, Elena let him grow his hair out to his ears. It flipped out by his face. Adam stilled but continued looking at his hands. From behind her desk, Mrs. Mathes cleared her throat before she began speaking.

"When Ms. White was singing her third song, Adam walked across the classroom and grabbed the guitar out of her hands, breaking her shoulder strap." Mrs. Mathes looked to the young teacher, whose tear-stained face stiffened when she realized that it was her turn to speak.

"Mrs. Phillips, he took my guitar from me and smashed it over his desk. It was a Taylor that my father bought me as a college graduation present."

"I'm so sorry, Ms. White. We're more than happy to replace the guitar for you," Elena interjected, mortified.

"That's very kind, but it's not replaceable." Ms. White's voice broke. "Adam is a wonderful boy, but . . ." she trailed off.

Mrs. Mathes cleared her throat, "We don't have the support that Adam needs here. I've contacted the district, and they've approved a move for Adam to our local day school."

"What do you mean?" Elena's chest crumpled at the news—what was a '"day school" anyway? Her son could no longer be in public school? She was shocked.

"The school is called Scott, and it's an accredited private school for students with special needs. Since our district doesn't have the resources, they will cover the cost of the school, which is accredited both by the National Council for Private Schools and the Catholic Conference Association. We prefer a secular school, but this is the best in the area, and I think Adam will find success there."

Elena spent the night sick with worry about yet another transition for her son. She managed to get him to sleep at nine o'clock, which was miraculous under normal circumstances but necessary for that day. She sat on the couch with Jon and took a deep breath. Her chest was tight with anxiety.

"I've been thrown out of better places than a public school," Jon said, trying to make a joke.

Elena couldn't laugh. "What are we supposed to do now?'

"We go to the day school tomorrow and check it out. It sounds like it could be a good idea. If we don't get a good vibe, we'll look into other options. Hey, the district is going to pay for a private school that we couldn't afford."

"It's Catholic, and we're not Catholic," Elena said.

"Even better. They'll work on his behavior and his soul," Jon quipped. "Everything happens for a reason, Laney. We've made it this far."

Elena knew that her husband was trying to comfort her, and she leaned into him. Men were always trying to figure things out and fix them, but right now Jon was just trying to support his wife. He was keeping her together, which she so desperately needed.

The next morning, she and Jon were taking Adam to meet with his new principal. Once they arrived at her office, they saw that it was the opposite of Mrs. Mathes's office. It was bright and cheerful. Ms. Rebecca Jones had a tree with the handprints of all of her students hung behind her desk, and she smiled and greeted the Phillipses warmly before sending Adam to the outdoor playground with an aide. Soft music played in the background as she spoke to Elena and Jon.

"Here's our usual day." Ms. Jones put a chart in front of the Phillipses. They were impressed with the colorful, blocked layout of the day, each time coordinated with an activity.

"At seven forty-five, the students all meet in the main hall where I greet them and we say prayers and the pledge of allegiance. At eight, they break off into their classrooms for two fifty-minute blocks of reading, followed by snack and recess at nine forty-five. We then break into our electives, lunch at noon, and a second recess. In the afternoons, students do computer lab, handwriting, and art for thirty-minute segments before being picked up at three o'clock."

"Wow," Jon said, looking at Elena. "This sounds like exactly the structure that Adam needs."

Elena relaxed into her seat a bit when she heard a knock on the door.

"Come in!" Ms. Jones called. When the door opened, she motioned another woman inside. "Mr. and Mrs. Phillips, this is Mona Jackson, our school caseworker from the county. She'll be evaluating Adam's progress every six months."

"Nice to meet you." Elena shook her hand. "But where is Lauren? She was our caseworker when we moved here."

"Lauren got married last year. She moved away. I'll be working with Adam now." Mona smiled.

While Elena was comforted by the new school's approach, she was still apprehensive about the changes. Then Ms. Jones guided her and Jon to a window where she could see Adam swinging with three other students. His face was tipped toward the sky, eyes closed and smile radiating pure joy.

CHAPTER 15
WAILING

Elena laughed as she sat across from Ms. Jones and Ms. Jackson in the conference room at the school. "I need a bumper sticker that says, 'My child is an honor student at Scott Therapeutic Day School.'" Adam had been attending the school for two years, and Elena had become very friendly with the principal and caseworker.

Ms. Jackson, the caseworker, laughed along with her. "He's doing so well," she agreed. "Eighth grade suits him. He's shown significant improvement and development of overall skills and even self-care skills—he still needs help but is more independent. Although he's still largely nonverbal and doesn't consistently use words meaningfully to communicate his wants and needs, he is communicating better with gestures and picture symbols."

"We've definitely seen improvement in those areas as well," Elena remarked, "but we're still having big problems with the meltdowns and tantrums at home."

"We have them here, too," Ms. Jones said. "But they're more manageable. As long as we can hold him with our arms, he eventually calms, finds himself again, and all is well in an hour or so."

An hour? Does she mean that they hold him for an hour or that it takes an hour for him to calmly resume activities back in class?

Just then, the phone buzzed. "Excuse me. Yes?" Ms. Jones answered her phone. "Yes." Her eyebrows knit with concern as she glanced at Elena. She listened for another minute. "Yes. I see. I have his mother here now. We'll be right down." She turned to Elena apologetically. "Could you come with me?"

Ms. Jones led Elena from her office and down the hallway. She talked as they walked. "Elena, that was Adam's teacher. Due to the snow, they're unable to play on the outside playground today, and as she was leading the class to the gymnasium, Adam shoved another student against the wall for no reason and then started banging his head against it. She was unable to restrain him, so she had to call in three aides from other classrooms to help. We have him in the nurse's office now."

Elena's adrenaline was suddenly coursing through her with maternal worry. Along with Ms. Jones, she rushed into the nurse's office, where Adam was pacing between the cots, eyes darting up at the ceiling. His forehead was coated in dried blood, and the nurse was sitting in her chair with rubber gloves on, waiting for him to settle.

"What's going on?" Elena exclaimed. "Adam, you need to sit down."

Adam looked up at the sound of his mother's voice and barreled toward her. An observer would have thought he was going to knock Elena over, but he pressed against her, lowering his head into her shoulder. Elena walked with him, guiding him to the cot where she managed to sit him down. She took the peroxide-soaked gauze from the table and started carefully dressing her son's wounds while whispering soothingly to him.

The next month passed in a haze of sleepless nights, the days running wildly together. The ringing of Elena's cell phone immediately set her nerves on edge; she seemed to startle more easily, and she thought she was beginning to understand how war veterans could spin into fight-mode at unexpected loud noises.

On an afternoon when Elena was trying to clean her neglected and cluttered house, her cell phone rang. She winced. "Hello, Ms. Jones," she answered.

"Elena, today has been a bad day. The meltdowns are just getting worse. Today he climbed the shelf in the reading area and jumped down on another student's back. We need to have a talk."

Half an hour later, Elena sat in Ms. Jones's office, tapping her foot.

"Elena, you know how much we love having Adam here," Ms. Jones said, "but—"

"No," Elena said. "No. Don't say it." Her heart pounded. She knew what was coming. She knew that apologetic, almost embarrassed tone.

"The meltdowns are seemingly without cause," Ms. Jones said, almost pleadingly. "They come out of the blue, and we can't find the antecedents or triggers. We also can't seem to determine the function or the reason for the behavior. Our team has thought that the function of the tantrums could be attention, or maybe task avoidance, but our interventions have not worked. This makes the meltdowns impossible for us to address, and Adam is putting other students and our staff at risk. I have a responsibility to—"

"You also have a responsibility to Adam," Elena said, fighting outraged tears. "He deserves an education just like every other child."

"You're absolutely right," Ms. Jones said, passing a box of Kleenex across her desk, which Elena ignored. "But we simply don't have the resources to support him here. I'm very sorry. This is unusual for us."

"So what exactly are you telling me, Ms. Jones?"

"We think that Adam would make better educational progress if he were home-schooled," Ms. Jones said. "It's a familiar environment, and we can offer you an in-home teacher to supplement his studies. She could come to your home, three times a week, for two hours."

Elena put her head in her hands. "A new routine and a different schedule each day won't work for Adam," she argued. "You know that. That's probably why he's been melting down lately—with the snow these last few days, he hasn't been able to go outside and swing. He can't take change, he never has, and I'm not qualified to educate my son—my severely delayed and autistic son."

"The teacher is certified in special education, has experience with autism, and can help you develop behavioral and educational strategies for working with Adam at home." Ms. Jones's voice quieted and broke a little, indicating that this was not an easy decision for her to make.

Elena was completely at a loss. She had no idea where to turn, so she didn't say another word. Instead, she rose from her chair, retrieved her son from the front office, and carried his lunch box, coat, and school supplies to the car. There, she strapped Adam into the backseat, sat behind the steering wheel, and cried like a child. Adam, sensing his mother's desperation, joined her. The wailing of mother and son filled the mini-van for a good fifteen minutes before Elena dried her eyes, smiled at Adam in the rearview mirror, and shifted the van into reverse.

CHAPTER 16
HOME-SCHOOL

Monday morning, Elena woke up resolved to make her son's life as similar to school as she could. She didn't have a playground, but she'd purchased all the same materials that the school used—workbooks were shipped overnight from Amazon, she bought the same CDs of relaxing music that they played during art time, and she prepared spaghetti before Adam woke up so it would be ready for his lunch without having to wait. She helped him get dressed and brush his teeth before she sat him at the dining room table.

"Adam, this is going to be like school, only Mommy will be working with you." She spoke plainly and clearly, just as she'd heard countless teachers and therapists work with her son. She displayed the American flag that she'd purchased on the table and stood with her hand over her heart.

"I pledge allegiance, to the flag . . ." Elena's heart swelled when she saw her son awkwardly put his right hand to his chest. Maybe this is crazy enough to work, she thought as she finished the pledge and pulled out her chair next to Adam's.

"We're going to start with reading." Elena pulled out the same workbook Adam had been using in school. She would primarily be reading to him, but the goal was to get him to understand how to interact with the book. To turn the pages and identify letters on the page as words. "You left off with lesson thirty-three, Peter Rabbit."

Adam started rocking in his seat, and when Elena looked over his head was bowed and his hands folded on the table.

"What's wrong, sweetie?" Elena asked, perplexed. "Now we read."

His rocking got more intense.

Elena racked her brain, trying to remember what he would have done at school that would prompt this. Then it hit her—he was enrolled in a Catholic school. They started the day with the pledge and a prayer. Elena's face flushed. She hadn't been to mass since Adam's baptism almost fourteen years earlier. She knew he could never sit through the service, and frankly, with the hand she'd been dealt, she wasn't sure where God fit into her life anymore. After all, where had He been all these years? She put her hand on top of his clasped fingers. "Would you like to pray the Our Father?"

Adam looked up at her and then quickly away, closing his eyes.

"Our father who art in heaven, hallowed be thy name," Elena started hesitantly. "Thy kingdom come, Thy will be done, on earth as it is in heaven. Give us this day . . ." Amazed, she watched as Adam's hand touched his right shoulder then this left—his version of the holy cross. Something reached him! Elena wiped tears from her eyes quickly, so that Adam didn't notice, and started reading to him.

The next week went much the same, with Adam working on his schoolwork after morning pledge and prayer. Elena was getting him settled with his number magnets to work on math when the phone rang. "You make numbers. Mommy will be right back," she told her son as she got up to answer the phone.

"Hello?"

CRASH! BOOM! Oh God, I should have known better than to disrupt his routine.

Elena hit the END button before the caller had a chance to speak and rushed back into their dining room, where she found Adam under the table banging his head against the leg. The dining room table shook from the impact before she heard the sickening crack of the leg giving way. In the next moment, the table that seated eight fell on top of her son. After the crash of the table, there were a few seconds of stunned silence before Elena heaved the heavy wood off her son. As soon as he was free of the table, his wail pierced through her house.

Elena tried pulling Adam to her, but he would not be comforted. He shoved her off and she slammed into the wall, hitting her head and biting her tongue. She was next to the house phone, which she quickly grabbed and dialed Jon at work.

"You need to come home, now!" she tried to keep her voice steady.

"What's going on?" Jon's voice was concerned.

Resigned, Elena said, "Adam is finally stronger than me."

"On my way."

When she hung up, she looked up to see that Adam was hyperventilating. Her motherly instinct took over, and she rushed to her son's side, squeezing his shoulders the best she could; he'd always been comforted by deep pressure. But today he wrenched away, slapping her across the face as hard as he could. Elena was knocked back into a seated position on the floor next to him. Adam lunged toward her, but she managed to get up and run into her bedroom. She stood with her back to the locked door, closed her eyes, and tried to breathe again. She heard Adam's tantrum move from the dining room into the kitchen, the banging of her stainless steel cookware against the granite of their countertops, the dishwasher door slamming open and shut. Then the noises retreated into the family room. Elena wanted to open her door slowly and creep in to see what he was destroying, but her feet stayed planted firmly on the ground. Her body wouldn't let her move until the beep of the alarm ten minutes later indicated that Jon was home.

"Elena?" he called. "Adam?"

Elena chanced to open the bedroom door and venture down the hallway. Her house looked as though a tornado had struck. The dining table was broken and leaning against a wall, her pots and pans were strewn throughout the kitchen, and her leather couch had a dent on the side where it had been kicked. Jon stood on the other side of the couch, his face in utter disbelief. All was quiet, and she was worried about Adam. What was I thinking, locking myself in my room? He might have really hurt himself. She walked over to her husband to see what he was looking at—Adam curled up in a ball on the floor, fast asleep.

Jon and Elena worked to get the house picked up and in some sort of order while Adam slept. They pulled the dining table out to the garage so that Jon could see if it could be salvaged. She put all of her pots and pans away, silently thanking God that Adam hadn't grabbed a knife while he was in the kitchen, while Jon swept up pieces of the glass picture frames that were thrown off the wall. They couldn't yet speak to each other about what happened. They each had to hold their stories in their hearts until they could find the words to articulate what was going on with their family. Jon called into work and said that he couldn't be there the next day. He simply didn't feel comfortable leaving Elena home alone with their son. Eventually, he'd have to find a way, but Adam needed to go back to the psychiatrist first thing in the morning.

Adam's three-hour nap, coupled with the Abilify, made his insomnia worse that night, and Elena found herself in bed with him again. She wrapped her arms around her son, trying to lull him to sleep with the pressure, and realized that her hands didn't reach all the way around him anymore. She wondered what would become of her son, now that he was obviously no longer her little baby. He'd never had a meltdown of these proportions before. Today's reality made her stomach turn. Just then, she felt the bed shift as Adam rolled over. The alarm clock on his bedside table read 3:17 a.m. She'd be lucky to get three hours of sleep.

When Adam finally dozed off at four a.m., Elena snuck back to her own bed but was unable to sleep. Watching her husband's back fall up and down with his steady breath made her crazy with envy. Her tears collected between her face and pillow and flowed onto her shoulder when she finally rolled over to stare at the wall. When her eyes finally stayed shut, she didn't dream but had a vision of being taken away in an ambulance with her daughter. In her vision, Shannon's sobs echoed over anything the EMTs were saying, and while Elena was terrified, she was relieved that Shannon was actually crying—actually grieving and letting something out.

CHAPTER 17
SEA OF DOUBT

Dr. Valentino crossed her legs as Elena recounted the previous day. Jon had stayed home to purchase and set up a new dining room table, and Adam was watching his iPad on the couch, headphones over his ears as Elena tearfully relived the worst afternoon of her life.

"I think we need to increase the Abilify," Dr. Valentino said.

"What?" Elena protested. "But what about the mood swings and the insomnia? I can't take much more of this, doctor. You said there would be improvement, and all we've seen is worsening of the meltdowns."

"You have to trust me, Elena. The FDA recently approved the drug for autism-related agitation. I think his dose isn't in the optimal range. I can also give you a mild sedative to improve Adam's sleep." She wrote out the prescriptions on her pad and handed the notes to Elena. "My recommendation? Adam's favorite dinner at your new dining table. After bath and bedtime, a glass of wine for Mom. These days are hard, but you'll get through them."

Elena was skeptical but chose to trust the doctor's advice; what other choice did she have? Hopefully the medication would help. It was her only option—wasn't it? She was drowning in a sea of doubt. Every time Adam moved his arms, she flinched—a kneejerk reaction to his hitting her.

Driving back from Dr. Valentino's office was a challenge. Adam had long since outgrown his safety booster and had to wear a regular seatbelt. The scratchy belt on his neck bothered him, so he fought to get out of the car. Though the child safety locks were always on, it nonetheless induced panic when her son slammed his shoulder against the car door or threw his fists into the window.

"Adam, calm," she said from behind the wheel. "Calm." God, what if he hits me while I'm driving? He could knock me out and possibly kill us both. The thought, unbidden, filled her with a white rush of fear. I just need to get us home.

That night, Elena plastered on a fake smile at Jon's new furniture decision and went to work in the kitchen. She had thawed out the chicken breasts even before Dr. Valentino recommended making Adam's favorite dinner, and as she cut them into strips to brine them in her apple cider vinegar mixture, she thought about how much she loved to be able to love on Adam, even if it was only through food. She set the thermometer into the grease and floured her chicken strips. When the oil hit 425, she started to dip them into the pan. She was so tired that the smell of the hot oil bubbling, cooking the meat, and browning the flour, was the only thing she could focus on. Maybe I'll sit down, just for a minute. She pulled out the barstool and rested her head on the island. The granite was cool on her cheek, and before she could get control of herself, she drifted off.

Smoke filled the room when Elena picked up her head. "Elena! Elena!" She heard Jon's voice through the fog, then a struggle and the banging of a metal lid over the big frying pan on the stove.

"What the hell? Were you trying to kill us?" Jon was yelling as he turned off the stove, and Elena saw their children standing in the dining room, wide-eyed. Shannon had a protective arm around Adam as he started to fidget, indicating that a meltdown was imminent. And who could blame him? His mother had just fallen asleep with a pan full of hot grease on the stove; talk about negligent. She didn't have time to berate herself fully, as Jon was right up in her face. "Where are you right now in your head? Are you there? Elena, are you ever in there anymore? I really wish you'd use your brain every once in a while."

Elena's eyes filled with tears as her husband judged everything about her with his anger and questions, but she exploded instead of crying.

"I'm here. I'm always the one who's here. If I downplayed your role in this family as much as you downplayed mine, you'd leave me!" she yelled at her husband. "Every day, I not only run this house, making sure everyone has clean clothes and meals, but I also educate our son, which is no small feat considering I'm not a teacher! Thanks for making money so that I can do everything else!" Elena was so angry that she didn't even notice Shannon guide Adam back into his bedroom. Her eyes achieved laser focus on her husband's, daring him to come back at her.

"I'm going to go and get our family some dinner." Jon's expression didn't change. "I'll be back in a little while."

He grabbed his car keys and wallet from the kitchen countertop and walked to the garage door.

"Don't!" Elena called after him, deflated from her outburst and devastated that he didn't even care enough to fight with her anymore.

"Elena, I don't have anything nice to say to you right now, so it's probably best that I don't say anything at all. If I open my mouth, I'll regret it. I'll bring home some chicken." Jon turned and walked out of the house.

Elena made it to the couch and flopped herself down. Her life was falling apart, and it all centered around the little boy she and Jon had talked about since their wedding night. He was so wanted, and she tried so hard to take good care of him. What had they done to deserve this? Why was life being so unfair?

The next day was Saturday, and although Elena and Jon had barely spoken more than two words to each other in the past twenty-four hours, Elena decided to mend fences with at least one member of her family. She was taking Shannon out to lunch, the first time the two of them had been out together in at least six months. As they were seated at the bistro, Elena thought twice about ordering a glass of sauvignon blanc and ultimately decided against it.

"How's school, darling?" Elena asked her daughter after the waiter took their drink orders. The restaurant was the kind designed for mother-daughter lunches: round tables could seat two, intimately, and the dining room looked as though it was in an old living room. Funky paintings adorned the walls, with small notes indicating they were for sale by local artists. The menu was complete with a variety of gourmet salads and soups, and the smell of freshly baked bread hit their noses as soon as they opened the door.

"It's great, Mom." Shannon was already a junior in high school. "My class load is challenging, but I love all my theory and composition classes. It was good to exclude Advanced Placement calculus this year, although I'm enjoying AP language and composition."

"I'm so glad to hear that." Elena smiled at her daughter, taking in her beauty in a way she hadn't been able to do lately. She was surprised at the young woman sitting in front of her. Shannon's hair was long and still had the wavy bounce to it that Elena had always wished her own hair possessed. Her green eyes shone in her olive complexion, and her posture and manners were immaculate. Elena gazed adoringly at her daughter. "I know we don't get to talk much . . ." she started, feeling a lump rise to her throat.

Shannon smiled at her mom. "It's okay, Mom. Hey, listen—I've been offered the opportunity to be the musical director for the community theatre's production of Little Shop of Horrors—"

"A musical director! Shannon, that's great!"

"—but I'm going to turn it down."

"What?" Elena asked. "Why?"

"Well, the rehearsal schedule is long, and I don't want to get behind on my studies." Shannon looked down, indicating that she wasn't telling the truth.

"Honey, look at me," Elena said. "You can get a 'B,' especially if it's because you're doing something fun. Why don't you tell me the real reason you're turning down the show?"

Shannon sighed, her shoulders rising with the breath. "Well, it's a long rehearsal schedule. I'd be gone most evenings until ten or eleven, and I—" Shannon motioned to the bruises on her mother's arm. She was afraid to leave Elena alone with Adam.

"Oh God, don't worry about me!" Elena laughed. "I'm a tough broad. I got this."

"Mom, I know that 'tough broad' and 'I got this' are things you say in jest, but your voice and face are always expressionless. I know it's from working with Adam, but I cannot read you anymore. It's impossible to connect with you because I don't ever know where you are! You just seem like you're somewhere else all the time. I'm really worried about you. I love you, Mom." Shannon took a moment to compose herself, but she looked as though she'd released a weight off her chest.

Elena's eyes filled with tears as she reached over to hold her daughter's hand across the table. "I love you too, sweetheart. You're right," she said heavily. "The only emotion I seem to feel these days is sadness. I'm really, really tired, Shannon. I can't imagine how all this has affected you. My God, I shouldn't be burdening you with this."

Shannon looked down, obviously a little embarrassed by her mother's guilt-ridden admission. "It's okay, Mom. I'll take a pass on the play. I really want to spend more time at home with my family."

CHAPTER 18
MARTYRING

The week after Adam's fifteenth birthday, Elena rummaged around in the pantry, searching for a box of spaghetti noodles she was sure she'd stuck away. She couldn't believe she'd run out, but when she reached the back shelf empty-handed, she knew she'd have to make Adam something else for dinner. Jon was working late, and she was just making the kids sandwiches after another long day at home with Adam. She found some ham in the refrigerator, slathered mayonnaise on the bread, and topped it with a slice of Swiss cheese. She brought the plates to the table, where Adam was watching *Barney* on his iPad. "Now we put away the iPad and we eat," Elena said to her son, putting his sandwich in front of him. He gripped the sides of the iPad, still gazing intently at the screen.

"No, Adam," she reached for the device, but he wouldn't let it go. "Fine," she released it. "You can watch *Barney* and eat, just tonight." She slunk into the chair next to him, calling, "Shannon, come eat!"

She was chewing the first bite of her food when a crash made her leap from her seat. Adam had bread crumbs on his shirt, indicating that he'd taken a bite of the sandwich and was unhappily surprised by the ham. His plastic plate lay upside down on the floor, a smear of mayo on the wall.

"Adam, no!" Elena stood to get the plate. "If you don't want to eat, that's fine, but don't throw the plates!" She bent over to pick up the pieces of plate from the carpeted floor when she felt Adam grab her from behind. He hurled her to the floor, sat on her chest, and started hitting her with his fists. At first, she felt the blows on her chest, but they soon moved up to her face.

In the distance, Elena heard Shannon screaming, "Adam, get off!" She heard the phone and was sure she heard Shannon talking to a 911 operator.

Less than ten minutes later, three police officers burst into the living room. Adam had lost interest in hitting Elena but had gone on a rampage, ripping pictures off the walls and breaking them on the tile. Elena was a mess—still on the floor—as she just couldn't find the will to stop him. Shannon was next to her mother, putting ice on her swelling face.

The EMTs were right behind the police, and while six police officers tried to wrestle Adam to the ground, one of the EMTs was waiting with a shot of sedatives. The other paramedic came to Elena's side, checking out her injuries.

"You're going to be just fine, ma'am. But what happened?" the young man asked Elena.

"My son is autistic. He lost control. Please, be gentle with him. He's scared and doesn't know what's going on."

"I think you both need to go to the hospital," said the EMT, his face solemn.

"I'm fine. Really." Elena pulled herself up, rushing to Adam. "I'm just worried about him."

All six police officers were on top of Adam while the EMT injected the third dose of sedative. Adam shook and fought, but was then still, snoring quietly almost immediately. The whole room breathed a collective sigh of relief.

Elena looked over at Shannon. "Grab my purse, sweetie. We're going to follow the ambulance." After being cleared medically at the local emergency room, Adam was transported by the police to the psychiatric hospital.

Elena called Jon on the way to the hospital, and he took off to meet them there. When he saw his wife's swollen, purple face, he burst into tears. He embraced his trembling daughter and wife in the waiting room, and none of them moved until an emergency room doctor came out to clear Adam for transport to Valleyview Hospital.

At Valleyview's psychiatric unit, another doctor met them in the waiting room after briefly evaluating Adam. "The Phillips family?"

"That's us." Jon pulled away from his family, wiping his eyes.

"Adam is sleeping still, but we'd like to keep him here for the next forty-eight hours. We want to make sure he's emotionally and behaviorally stable, not at risk of harming himself or others, and that his medications are working correctly."

Elena buried her face into Jon's jacket. Her tears came from not only a place of sadness, but also from a place of relief, which made her cry even harder. She couldn't believe that she was so happy to have her son out of the house for two days. She just felt so tired.

"Can we see him?" Shannon's voice was quiet.

"Right now is probably not a good idea. It's been a long day. Why don't you go home, get some rest, and then come back tomorrow?" The doctor smiled sadly at them and walked through the automatic doors towards the elevator.

The clock on the stove flipped to eleven p.m. as Elena stirred the Splenda into her tea. She'd made her favorite kind; if she couldn't sleep, at least she could have some comfort. She made her way out to her back porch and sat, listening to the spring cicadas. The sliding glass door opened, and Jon came out. "You couldn't sleep, either?" he asked.

"Nope." Elena looked up at her husband. Her eyes were swollen from Adam's blows and the tears that hadn't stopped for the past few years.

"Elena, we can't do this anymore—you can't do this anymore."

Elena's tears came again. "What other option do we have?"

Jon sat beside her and rubbed his eyes. "The one we've never talked about," he said, his voice heavy. "Laney, maybe Adam would do better in an environment staffed 24/7 by people who know how to work with him."

"A home?" Elena asked, gaping at her husband. "You want to put our son in a home?"

"A residential care setting, Elena. There are some good ones out there. I've done some research—"

"Because I'm doing such a terrible job?" Elena's voice rose. "Is that it? I should just send my baby to live with other people because I'm such a shit parent?"

"That's not what I'm saying at all, but look at who you've become—who we've become!" Jon tried to keep his voice calm but was mostly unsuccessful. "Why do you talk to me like this? How long has it been since you slept longer than an hour here and there? Adam, our son, beat the hell out of you! It's obvious. It's just not working and it's tearing us apart. It's tearing me apart!"

"No one will take care of Adam like I can. I'm his mother. We have a special bond. But you're saying I can't bring him through the world I brought him into? Do you know what it feels like to hear that?" Elena's voice cracked with emotion. Crying even harder, she continued, "I was the first voice he heard and the first to look into his beautiful eyes. The first to hold him and the first to fall in love with him. Do you have any idea how inadequate and powerless I feel? That despite all my efforts, my son wants to injure me?"

Jon's stony expression melted away. He'd never thought about Elena taking Adam's behavior as a failure on her part. "I'm sorry," he said. "But Laney, Shannon and I need you, too. It's not fair for any of us to continue repeating the past."

"But I have an obligation to him," Elena argued. "He's our child. He needs me. I can't turn my back on him."

"No one is asking you to. There are some great places, where Adam can get help."

"But—"

"You know what?" Jon interrupted, angrily shaking his head. "This is nuts, and you're starting to tick me off. You're my wife, Shannon's mother, and you're being selfish. Adam needs help—the kind we can't give him. Your thinking is denying him the treatment and care that he so desperately needs. Laney, he's fifteen! This isn't about what works best for you. See reality. You're not solving this problem, and acting like some kind of martyr isn't helping either."

For a few minutes, Elena just wept. She was heartbroken at his words and the anger behind them, but she also felt a sense of relief. Jon was right—she was martyring herself, completely neglecting any responsibilities she had to anyone except Adam. Her belief in this personal crusade and the idea that only she could adequately take care of her son was not helping him or anyone else. Maybe she didn't have to carry that burden in her heart anymore. Maybe Jon was right. "Okay," Elena whispered. "Let's look at some residential care programs."

Jon put his arm around his wife, and they stared at the sky together. Between them was an intimacy and closeness they hadn't remembered in years.

CHAPTER 19
PSYCHIATRIC UNIT

The alarm clock shone 2:47 a.m. into the darkness of the master bedroom. Jon turned and looked at Elena. His wife looked peaceful, breathing quietly. He kissed her gently on the forehead and moved a lock of dark hair from her eyes. He remembered when they first got married, how he'd stayed awake just to see the peace on her face while she slept. Quietly, he rolled out of bed, put on a pair of blue jeans and a t-shirt, and crept downstairs. The house was completely still as he made his way down to his workshop in the basement. He fumbled with the light switch and opened the refrigerator door, cracked open a beer, and listened to the rain coming down. The soft patter hit the grass, and it sounded sleety, as if winter were on its way. He knew that feeling. The weight in his heart echoed the heavy snow clouds that would soon be rolling into Wisconsin.

He worried a lot these days, about his family especially. His thoughts were consumed with his son's future, his daughter's college education, his wife's happiness, and, more recently, her emotional health. Silent tears streamed down his cheeks as he finished the beer.

He wiped his face as he went upstairs, looked out the front window, checked the door locks, and peeked in on Shannon, who was sleeping in the same position as her mother. Then he went into Adam's room and sat on his son's vacant bed, praying to God for answers. None came, but he had a feeling the questions were heard. Jon then went back to his bedroom, quietly pulled the blanket back, and laid down beside his wife, pushing his arm against hers. He kept his blue jeans and t-shirt on because that made it easier in the morning. Jon drifted off to sleep thinking about how hard he tried to be a good man . . . not a perfect man, by any stretch, but a good man just trying to take care of his family and do the right thing.

The next morning, Elena woke to the phone ringing. She looked over at her alarm clock. Nine-thirty. She and Jon had gone to bed around midnight, meaning that she'd slept for nine and a half hours. She looked around her room. Obviously, Jon and Shannon were off at work and school. The blaring ring of the phone was the only noise in the house, and Elena remembered the previous day. She closed her eyes and sighed before fumbling for the cordless phone next to her bed.

"Mrs. Phillips? This is Mary Henderson from the county. How are you this morning?"

"I'm fine, thank you," Elena replied.

"Good to hear. I'm calling about Adam. Right now he's in Pinehurst Hospital, correct?"

"Yes, ma'am."

"We're making a recommendation that he be discharged and sent to Valleyview. The psychiatric unit is better suited to him, and with the level of aggression that he displayed yesterday, we feel that an extended hospitalization might be necessary."

Elena's eyes filled with tears. She never thought she would consent to sending her son to a mental institution. God, the word just sounded so awful. But, after her talk with Jon, she knew something had to change. "Um, okay. What do we need to do?"

"We will have all of Adam's paperwork completed and sent through the system in time for his discharge tomorrow morning. We can send him in an ambulance if you'd like, or your family can take him."

"We'll take him," Elena said quickly. "Thank you for taking care of this for us. We appreciate your help."

"It's our pleasure, Mrs. Phillips. I'm Adam's caseworker now, so if you need anything at all, let me give you my cell number. Unfortunately, sometimes there are hiccups in the system, and I want tomorrow to go as smoothly as possible for you."

When Elena hung up the phone, she went into Adam's room to pack a suitcase for her son. As she pulled sweatpants from the closet and t-shirts from his dresser, she remembered doing his baby laundry. His clothes were so small that she could fit them in her hand. Now she had to remember whose was what so that she didn't confuse his clothes with Jon's. Silent tears fell as she balled up his last pair of socks. The chime of the house alarm, indicating that someone was home, broke her reverie.

"Hello?" she called out.

"It's me." Jon stepped into Adam's doorway. She could smell the motor oil on his skin as he walked over and embraced her. "What are you doing?" he asked softly.

"Getting Adam's things together. The county called. They want to transfer him to Valleyview."

"When?"

"Tomorrow morning. Our son will be in a psychiatric ward and not just for a forty-eight hour observation." The tears started falling more quickly and Elena's chest ached from all the crying she'd done in the past day.

Jon came to her and brushed his fingers over Elena's face, which was thankfully not as bruised as he'd anticipated, although there was still some swelling. "It's what we have to do, Elena. At least until we figure something else out."

"I know, it's just—it's just hard. The whole thing is impossible! We're good people, Jon. We don't deserve this. Adam doesn't deserve this."

"I know, baby. I know." Jon pulled his wife into his chest and could feel her back heaving with emotion. He wanted to fix this—he should have been able to fix this long ago. He hated to see his family torn apart, but he really hated the deterioration of his wife. He knew they were in a no-win situation: keep Adam at home and drive everyone apart, or send him away and break everyone's hearts. Right now, though, they all needed a little space, and he was thankful that the county would send Adam somewhere safe. At the hospital, he would receive the care he needed, and Elena could catch up on her rest, reenergize, and work on becoming a whole person again, not just the mother to a child with autism.

CHAPTER 20
ALL STORMS PASS

"Hey, buddy!" Elena exclaimed. She couldn't keep her voice down. As relieved as she was to have a day away from her son, she'd missed him terribly. Her identity had become completely wrapped up in him, and she'd found herself shifting in bed all last night, hearing phantom cries coming from his room.

From his hospital bed, Adam responded by flapping his hands.

"He's still under the influence of medication. We gave him a mild sedative for the car ride," the doctor explained.

Shannon rushed over to her brother's bedside. "I missed you, sweetie." She planted a kiss on his forehead and got a little giggle out of him. "Look! You're wearing your skateboard shirt! Super cool!" She'd opted to stay home from school that day so she could ride to the new hospital with her family. She'd missed Adam greatly while he was gone, too, and she most certainly didn't want to keep the image of him throwing punches at their mother in her mind any longer than she had to.

A male nurse came in with a wheelchair and helped Adam into it. "You ready, big guy?" he asked, using his heft to lift Adam's close to two-hundred pound body from the bed.

Jon was waiting out front with the car and quickly got out when he saw his family emerge from the sliding glass doors of the hospital. They put Adam in the back-seat of his Toyota 4Runner, sliding him to the middle so that Shannon and Elena could get in on either side of him.

Elena laced her fingers through her son's as soon as she buckled her seatbelt. She looked over and saw that Shannon had done the same. Both women leaned into Adam's shoulders, and he didn't resist their cuddles. Jon looked at his beautiful family from the rearview mirror as he shifted the car into drive. From this vantage point, they all looked perfect—not as though they were driving their son to spend time in a psychiatric ward but maybe to take family photos or go to the zoo. He had to shake off the thought; there was a purpose to everything, and Adam wouldn't stay there forever. He was just sure of it.

Elena kept her head on her son's shoulder for the en-tire forty-five minute drive to the next hospital. When Jon pulled to a stop in front of the facility, she looked at the patient drop-off area. Everything about it was just like any other hospital. There were nurses off to the side smoking cigarettes in their scrubs, and people coming in and out. As they approached the automatic glass doors leading into the lobby, she could already smell the disin-fectant that made the air heavy in every medical center. Reluctantly, she let go of Adam's hand to let them know they had arrived. When she pulled away, she saw Adam looking around, confused. Oh my God, he thought we were going home! The thought was too much for Elena, and she wept as she told the orderly at the front desk that Adam Phillips had arrived. The orderly gave her a sympathetic look and went around for a wheelchair.

"We have all his paperwork in order, Mrs. Phillips." The older woman patted her arm as she brought the wheelchair out front. "Your caseworker is persistent. Called three times to confirm."

That gave Elena a little hope as she walked out with the wheelchair. Shannon helped Adam out of the car and into the chair. Her brother was twice her size, but the feat only showed her devotion to him. Jon handed his keys over to the valet and stuck the slip in his wallet as he walked over to take the reins of the chair.

"I'd like to push him, if you don't mind," he said to the orderly.

"Not at all." The orderly smiled at Jon and stepped aside.

When they arrived at Adam's floor, Elena was surprised at the sterility of the hallway. She'd only been in the hospital twice—for the births of her children—but the only difference between that floor and this one was a lack of blue and pink ribbons hung on the doors. When Adam was born, she'd walked the hall with him, trying to calm him while they stayed in the hospital for forty-eight hours. She'd noticed that one room didn't have the blue or pink ribbon but a picture of a rainbow. "What's that?" she'd asked the nurse later.

"Their baby passed away. We hang rainbows on the door so that nurses remember before they enter. It's a promise that the storm will pass. All storms pass."

Elena clutched her nursing newborn even closer to her chest. She couldn't imagine what they were going through—surrendering a child when his life should just be beginning. But now she had a better idea than she'd ever wanted. Adam was fifteen. She should be fighting with him about getting his learner's permit or nagging him to finish his homework so that one day he could go to college and have a bright future. Instead, she was accompanying him to a hospital where he was going to stay indefinitely. She fought back her tears. She was weary from crying, but now she needed to be strong for her son.

When they got Adam settled in his room—which, thankfully, looked less sterile and more like the dorms Elena's girlfriends lived in during college—the doctor came in to introduce himself to the family.

"I'm Dr. DuPont," the balding man said. "I'll be one of the doctors taking care of Adam." He didn't extend his hand for a handshake or do much of anything except confirm Adam's medical history and leave.

Elena was shaken by his abruptness and had reservations about leaving until she met April, Adam's nurse. April sat on the bed next to him while taking his vitals. She spoke to him directly, explaining what she was doing in a clear, cheerful voice, before reassuring the family that she would take care of him as if he were her own. She then told the family that they should start saying their goodbyes but they were welcome to come back anytime between eight a.m. and six p.m. any day. The tightness in Elena's chest loosened a bit, and she embraced her boy, kissing his head and promising to return the next morning. She left the room to let Shannon and Jon say their goodbyes. She could no longer hold back the tears that had been building since she'd spoken to the orderly and didn't want Adam to see her upset.

The next morning, Elena returned to the hospital at eight thirty. She brought Adam's iPad and a pillow from his bed with her so that he would have something familiar. Her sweet boy was lying in the bed watching *Barney* when she walked in.

"Hi, baby." She bent down to kiss her son. He didn't notice her.

"Adam? Mommy's here," she said again. Still nothing. She hit the PAGE button, and April walked in the door just a minute later.

"Hi, Mrs. Phillips! How are you today?"

"I'm fine. Listen, Adam is less responsive than usual."

"Oh, it's the medication."

"What?"

"The medication. Dr. DuPont has him on a sedative."

"Why?"

"So that he doesn't become violent. He does have a history of that, right?"

"Well, yes, but not often. What's the next course of treatment?"

April looked around. "You'll have to talk to the doctor, but I'll be honest. There's not a firm course of treatment right now. The plan is to keep him as calm as possible."

Elena felt outraged. She'd not wanted to send her son somewhere where they kept him doped up all the time. That wasn't what she had in mind. "What can I do?"

April closed the door to the room and motioned to Elena to sit in a chair. "You and your husband should take a look at a residential school for kids with autism. One is Genesee Lake School. They're top of the line. It's the only place I'd send my own children."

"Where is it?"

"It is in Oconomowoc, Wisconsin. I can't talk long, but I'll write the name and address down. They're much better suited for a long-term care situation and out of home placement. Our job is to mostly make sure the individual is stable. Also, according to the Individuals with Disabilities Education Act, he's entitled to a free and appropriate education, which isn't going to happen here." April scribbled down some information and slipped it into Elena's hand. "Your caseworker is Mary Henderson, right? She's good. She'll do the best she can to get you a tour or some people to talk to."

April winked and walked out the door while Elena sat, stunned. She'd had no idea there were other possibilities for her son. While she desperately wanted to sit with him, she was equally desperate to find another option for him. She kissed him once more, left, and got into her car determined to investigate her options.

From her cell phone, she dialed Mary's cell number.

"Mary Henderson," the caseworker answered her phone.

"Yes, this is Elena Phillips."

"Hi, Mrs. Phillips." Mary's voice was warm. "How is Adam?"

"I just visited him, and he is all drugged up. A little bird told me about Genesee Lake School, and I was wondering if you could fill in the specifics."

"Of course—Genesee Lake School is a residential school for young people with disabilities. They have a specific program for lower-skilled children and youth with autism spectrum disorders. They also have several group homes. They're phenomenal."

"How did I never find out about this place?"

"Well . . . red tape and such. Plus budgets and funding to be honest." Mary's voice was embarrassed.

Never mind the drama, Elena thought. "Could we get Adam there?"

"The funding process is rarely as smooth as we'd like, but I promise I will do the best I can. Do me a favor—research the place online and talk it over with your husband. We'll set up a meeting with Ms. Jackson from Scott next week if possible."

"Thank you!" Elena was buzzing with relief. "I have to get him out of that hospital."

After ending her call with Mary, Elena immediately dialed Jon's number.

"Hello?"

"You have to come home! I found something that has potential for Adam—long term. It could be just what we're looking for. I have to go home and search for it, but I talked to April, the nurse, and then I called Mary, Adam's caseworker, and—"

"Slow down!" Jon said. "Where are you?"

"I'm driving home. I just went to see Adam, and they have him drugged out of his mind. He can't stay there. I started to raise hell with April when she told me about a school for kids like Adam. They also offer a group home setting. It's an hour away, but she said it's the only place she'd send her own kids. I'm going home to look it up now. If it looks promising, I'm going to schedule a tour for us to check it out. Adam just can't stay in the hospital. He can't!"

"I understand, Laney, but frankly, you sound a little manic."

"No, Jon, I'm excited. For once, I'm excited about a

prospect for our son if we aren't able to support him right now at home. I feel as if there's a light, you know?"

"Okay," Jon said, his own voice showing wary optimism. "Listen, look everything over. If you get a good vibe, schedule a tour. I can't leave early today, but I can take tomorrow off. We'll talk about it when I get home."

"Okay. I love you," she said absently.

"I love you, too." Jon closed his eyes. His wife hadn't said she loved him before hanging up the phone in years. She may have been talking a mile a minute, but at least some part of her was back to where she used to be.

Elena was overwhelmed when she opened her browser window. She saw the wide-open spaces on the campus and read about Genesee Lake School's philosophy of care. They were a therapeutic residential care setting, and the focus was on all areas of growth and development. The goal was to get him to a place where he could successfully return home, not simply be medicated into docility for the rest of his life. Adam would have a private room, with people qualified to take care of him around the clock. Elena called the number on the contact page and found herself spilling her life story to the admissions coordinator who answered the phone. The conversation was an emotional blur until she heard, "Yes, of course, Mrs. Phillips. We would love to see you tomorrow morning" from the other end of the line. Elena hung up the phone and dialed Jon.

"I hope you got the day off tomorrow, because our dreams for Adam just might be coming true."

PART III

CHAPTER 21
ADMISSIONS

Elena could hardly believe her eyes when she and Jon pulled up to the main center building at Genesee Lake School. Genesee Lake School, where Adam could receive residential therapeutic school services, was only a part of the larger whole of Oconomowoc Residential Programs. Middle Genesee Lake shone in the sun, surrounded by lush, green grass and tall trees, and Elena's heart smiled with relief at the contrast from the sterile hospital where her son lay highly medicated and staring at the television. She reached over and squeezed Jonathan's hand, and the warmth in his eyes reflected the melting in her chest. Jon parked the car, and Elena got out and looked around. The campus was huge, and although it was in a rural area on the outskirts of a beautiful, historical town, the buildings looked modern, the brick sides resembling those of the performing arts high school that Shannon attended.

Jon walked over to the passenger's side of the car and put his hand into Elena's. "Not bad, eh?"

Elena smiled. "So far, so good. Let's go inside."

They walked into the building, which reminded Elena

of the fancy main halls in the colleges her girlfriends had attended almost twenty years ago. A receptionist was sorting paperwork but looked up to greet the Phillipses with a smile.

"You must be the Phillips family!" She stood to shake each of their hands.

"We are." Elena smiled, a little taken aback. She hadn't expected such a warm reception.

"I'm Val. Carl, our admissions coordinator, is waiting for you. I'll let him know that you're here. Just have a seat over there." Val motioned to the maroon colored leather couches in the waiting room.

Elena and Jon sat down, but before either of them could pick up a magazine to flip through, a big man whose smile shone as brightly as his balding head came through the double doors.

"Jon and Elena? Hello, I'm Carl, the Genesee Lake School admissions coordinator." He walked over to the couple, hand extended.

Jon stood and shook Carl's hand, while Elena smiled and followed him to Carl's office. The light grey of his walls reflected the sunlight coming in through his picture window, giving everything a dream-like appearance. Elena had been so excited to get Adam out of the hospital, but she hadn't imagined he could go somewhere where they remembered her family by name before they'd even met. She glanced around the office—the posters hanging on the wall were inspirational but far from cheesy. Elena sat next to Jon in the black padded chairs opposite Carl, his desk between them.

"I understand from our phone call that you're interested in learning more about Genesee Lake School and how it might fit the needs of your son, Adam." Carl smiled. "Can you tell me more about Adam?"

Elena looked at Jonathan. "Well, I'm not sure where to start." She giggled nervously.

"I understand he's presently at Valleyview Psychiatric Hospital?" Carl asked.

"Yes. He's—" Elena's voice broke. "He had a violent outburst, we had to call the police, and one thing led to another so that the police recommended he be placed in a hospital." She wiped her left eye with her fingertip to avoiding smudging her eyeliner. Since Adam had been gone, she'd been wearing makeup daily, and adjusting to her new reflection was a revelation each time she caught a glimpse of herself in the mirror. While the crow's feet at the corners of her eyes had grown considerably longer, she lacked the black rings around her eyes that came from long nights without sleep.

Jon cut in. "He's currently at Valleyview because his outburst led to Elena's swollen face. It was the only time he's ever been like that, and it's our belief that it was just a perfect storm of things in his life to lead him there. Adam is, for the most part, very kind and sweet."

Carl smiled, not the condescending smile that Jon and Elena were accustomed to when they tried to praise their son in front of other people. He seemed genuine, and Elena felt that he would have Adam's best interests at heart, just as she did.

"Tell me more. Where is he currently enrolled in school?"

"He's not," Elena said. "That's part of the problem. I've been home-schooling him for the better part of a year now. He was at a day school, but they couldn't figure out how to prevent his meltdowns, so they told me that home-schooling Adam was the best option."

"Were the police involved with his hospitalization?" Carl asked.

"Yes. No charges were pressed."

Elena was feeling uncomfortable diving right in with all the worst information on Adam, so she changed the subject. "Can you tell me how Genesee Lake School works with students with autism spectrum disorders? In particular, autistic disorder?"

Carl nodded. "Of course, I'd be happy to do that. Many of our children and youth at GLS with autistic disorder are served within our ICARE program. ICARE refers to Innovative Care for Autism and Related Disorders. In the ICARE program, our residential and educational staff, including occupational and speech therapy, follow a DIR framework across the residential therapeutic milieu and the special education classroom. DIR refers to the Developmental, Individual Differences, Relationship-Based model for autism and related disorders. Are you familiar with DIR?"

Elena's eyes lit up. "Yes! I saw that on your website, and it was part of what attracted me to your program. I tried to read all of Stanley Greenspan's books when Adam was young. Plus, Adam's occupational therapist always said that she followed DIR principles like Floortime in her work with Adam."

"Whatever she was doing," Jon added, "it sure seemed to work for Adam. I remember Lyndsey always told me to pay attention to his cues, or something like that."

Carl smiled and nodded. "Yes, Adam's occupational therapist was working to establish a positive relationship with Adam, paying attention to his cues, using his natural interests, and essentially taking his lead during play-based interactions in order to create a shared experience, to build upon his social emotional skill development. Anytime you can create a shared experience with a child with autism, who is often self-absorbed, and actually create an interaction around the experience—well, you are doing really good work. DIR requires flexibility on the part of the caregiver and really paying attention to the child's cues or what he tells us through his behavior. If Adam attends GLS, our ICARE staff will need to get to know him better—his likes, dislikes, and interests. Then we would use those interests and take his lead to build in fun and play-based Floortime interactions to develop skills. Adam is older," Carl added, "and it does take time—but as Dr. Greenspan believed, and we do, too, it's never too late to strengthen developmental foundations in relating, communicating, and thinking."

It's never too late. The words rang joyfully in Elena's head. "What's the daily routine like here?" she asked.

"If Adam attends GLS, he will participate in our special education school program during the day and then the residential therapeutic milieu the rest of the time," Carl said. "In the ICARE program, we serve both boys and girls. We have six ICARE classrooms with a capacity of seven children per room, and each classroom has a certified special education teacher, an instructional aide, and additional educational support staff. After school, children in ICARE live in one of five residential groups, with a staffing pattern of one adult for three children. Adam would be in the boys group that is the best fit given his age and skill level. Right now, I think it would probably be our Vista group." Carl paused for a moment, to see if Jon and Elena had any questions. When Jon slightly nodded, indicating for Carl to go on, he continued.

"The ICARE program also uses the SCERTS model, which is a comprehensive, multidisciplinary educational approach designed for children with autism spectrum disorders. SCERTS refers to social communication, emotion regulation, and transactional supports, and the model is very compatible with DIR. In the ICARE program, we also always remember that behavior is a form of communication, and behavioral problems are a form of expression. We also believe that family involvement in a child's care is vital for his success and successful transition home. We see kids on a developmental ladder, and it takes teaching skills over time to help him move up the rungs."

While a bit overwhelmed by all the information, the final analogy struck Elena beautifully. Adam was on his way up—not his way out.

"I know that was a lot of information," Carl said with a smile. "But the overall message is that we believe it's never too late to strengthen developmental foundations, and that is best achieved through positive relationships that develop skills to last a lifetime, so that children and youth in our care can successfully return to their home, school, and community. Let's take a walk around," he added, standing. "I'll show you the school building and the residential living areas—and seriously, if you have any questions, please feel free to ask."

"Sounds great, and yes, I'm sure we will have questions," Jon said with a laugh, thinking of all the information to digest.

Carl led them through the main building to the ICARE classrooms. Through the glass window, the family could see the rectangular-shaped tables in the lower lit room. Scattered throughout the room were sensory tools, rubber balls with blunt spikes protruding through the skin, metallic tangles that could be manipulated into various shapes, and fuzzy blocks with numbers one through nine on them. Three boys and a girl sat at one table, each with his or her own aide. A boy who was close to Adam's stature was leaning back into his one-on-one aide, and the man had his arms wrapped tightly around the boy's shoulders, mimicking what Jon had done with his son many times. A big man walked towards Jon and Elena beyond the doorway.

"This is Will, one of the ICARE clinical coordinators," Carl said, as Will exited the classroom. "Clinical coordinators are responsible for case management and service coordination. He's responsible for our individualized treatment plans, including skills assessment and intervention."

Will smiled at Jon and Elena, said hello, and shook each of their hands. He was easily six foot four, taller than even Jonathan was. His broad shoulders and big hands were intimidating until Elena looked into his big brown eyes; their warmth reminded her of Shannon's old teddy bears.

"This is one of our ICARE classrooms," Will said. "We keep the lighting low because some of the kids can become over-stimulated by bright lights. Also, traditional fluorescent light can be distracting and dysregulating for our students. You'll see that each student is matched with an adult so that everyone gets the interaction and individual attention they need to learn. We use sensory tools to assist with regulation and engagement in academic tasks with our students." Will smiled at Jon and Elena as one of the students in the classroom let out a yell, slapping the table with his palm. "Would you like to hear more specifics about ICARE?"

"We'd like that very much," Jon smiled as Will led the family down the hallway to his office. Will pulled an information folder from his desk and started to explain the program.

"Within thirty days of admission, we would put together an individual treatment plan that outlines initial goals and objectives during his placement at GLS. The assessment for the treatment plan includes behavioral and play-based observation, data collection, parent and staff interviews, review of records, and a team-based assessment of functional development levels. The treatment plan will include a sensory motor profile, comfort zone activities, objectives, and specific techniques and approaches to develop social emotional skills through the DIR model—areas such as shared attention and regulation, engagement and relating, purposeful communication, shared problem solving, and eventually emotional thinking."

"I hope this helps because Adam's been tearing the place up," Jon remarked.

Elena shot her husband a look.

"Kids often come here with very significant behaviors," Will said. "We have found that the treatment plans focusing on developmental levels and sensory needs have an increased impact on those challenging behaviors. It's always important to understand that GLS is able to offer our kids something that they seem to thrive on—structure, consistency, routine, visual supports, and a good old fashioned 'autism friendly' environment. Behavioral problems also improve through staff having a better understanding of each child's developmental skill level, which then contributes to a more compassionate understanding of challenging behavior. So a skills deficit—often related to language and communication impairment or maybe an unregulated sensory system—is the primary reason for challenging behavior. We also use more specific functional behavioral assessment approaches to develop behavior support plans with antecedent, teaching, and responding strategies for significant challenging behavior that persists and is not responding to our general environmental and therapeutic approaches. In the school program, we also offer year-round special education with IEP-related occupational therapy, speech therapy, and adaptive physical education. In ICARE, many of our kids use augmentative communication devices, like voice output device technology. Also, our consulting child and adolescent psychiatrist works within our health services department and monitors all medication."

"Wow," Elena said. "Everything looks and sounds so great." She was smiling at the prospect of this comprehensive care for her Adam.

"If we were in a room filled with every imaginable thing, toy, or object under the sun, what would Adam pick to play with? What would he be interested in?" Will asked.

"A swing set, without a doubt," Elena said instantly. "Monkey bars, even though he's getting too big for any at a playground now. His iPad, so that he can watch *Barney* and listen to his music. He's a big Cher fan, and can bust a move to 'Gypsies, Tramps and Thieves.'" Elena chuckled at the memory of Adam shaking his booty to the song when it randomly came on the radio one afternoon. His big legs trembled under his weight as he got down, the biggest smile stretched across his face.

Will made notes as Elena spoke. "Great. So he finds those things meaningful; we will keep that in mind as we prepare for his possible admission. If he attends GLS, the staff would use some of those ideas to foster engagement and back and forth communication, create shared experiences, and ultimately better relationships. Does he have any food intolerances or food allergies?"

"No allergies, but he's very particular about what he eats." Elena sighed. "He would live off fried chicken and spaghetti. He must be pretty hungry in the hospital, as I'm sure they don't give him what he wants all the time."

Will nodded. "Tell me more about how he handles frustration. Do you see any patterns when it comes to him getting angry? Any common triggers?"

"Change is a trigger, or not getting what he expected. The last meltdown that we had—the big one—was because we were out of spaghetti noodles so I made him a ham sandwich. Any abrupt interruption is also a trigger. You know with most kids you can tell them to turn off the TV and come eat dinner or take a bath? We can't with him. We have to transition him gradually out of TV and into dinner. Otherwise, he will have a meltdown."

"What are some signs that he is about to go into meltdown mode? What exactly do you see him do prior to a meltdown? If I were a fly on the wall, what would I see during these times?"

"Well, he kind of hops from one foot to the other." Jon stood to demonstrate, bouncing as he shifted his weight from his left to his right foot. "He'll also make noises. He doesn't say many words, but he he'll give a groan that indicates he's at his limit. It all happens pretty quickly, and then he's in full meltdown mode, maybe attacking people or hitting his head on the floor."

"Sounds like you know your son well. You've paid attention to his cues," said Will.

"Well, as the parent of a child with special needs—and autism, in particular—you learn to pay attention to everything," replied Elena.

"How do you help support him during these times?"

"When he's out of control?" Jon asked, and Will nodded. "We noticed that it helps if we wrap our arms around him, kind of around his upper arms, and squeeze tight as tightly as we can," Jon said. "I have more success than Elena does, now that he weighs more than she does. But he likes to be held close. If he's on his own, he'll tug on the bottom of his hoodie. He has a special jacket that he wears most of the time, and he'll pull the bottom of it down as far as he can. We've had to replace it often, as he'll pull the bottom seam right out. Good thing our son has an affinity for a plain, Hanes hoodie that we can replace at Target." Jon smiled.

"Good," Will said. "So it sounds like deep pressure helps him regulate better, and when he's on his own, pulling on his hoodie helps, too. Now, if Adam does come to GLS, our occupational therapists would like to see all reports and evaluations you have so we can use it to create his treatment plan. Do you have any other questions right now?"

"I don't think so," Elena said, looking at Jon.

"Great. I'll walk you back to Carl's office now. I hope to meet your son soon," Will finished, smiling.

"Yes, I hope so, too." Elena smiled back, although the hope thrown into the conversation had thrown her for a loop. She'd been so caught up in all the new information—the new ideas, the beautiful campus and friendly staff—that her mind had been working in terms of when Adam gets here as opposed to if Adam gets here.

Fifteen minutes later, Carl wished Elena and Jon well and opened the lobby door for them. The couple walked back to their car in silence. They got in, buckled their seatbelts, and Jon shifted the car into gear before Elena finally spoke. "It's great." Her voice was little more than a whisper.

"It is," Jon agreed. "I'm glad you said it, because I didn't want to. I was afraid I would jinx it if I wanted it too much."

Elena allowed herself a laugh. "You silly, superstitious man." She looked down at her hands. "I felt the same way."

"What are you doing?" Jon asked Elena as she scrolled through her phone's contact list.

"I'm calling Mary Henderson. I love this place. It feels right for Adam, and we're going to try to work out this funding issue as soon as possible."

An hour later, they pulled into their garage with two Sonic cherry limeades and an appointment with Mary Henderson.

CHAPTER 22
SILENT PRAYER

Six weeks later, Elena got into her car and got on the interstate. She was heading back home from a visit with Adam at the hospital. As much as she missed her son, she needed a day to herself, so she only spent a few hours with him that morning. She walked into her empty house and kicked her shoes off in the laundry room right off the garage door. She walked into the living room, where she plopped herself on the couch with her laptop and clicked on the bookmarked link to Genesee Lake School's website. The past six weeks had been nonstop. Mary was cooperative, but her superiors had proven anything but. Jon and Elena had to dip back into their Discover card to hire a special needs attorney—at an expensive retainer—to bring their case to the county. There were days she could only spend a few hours with Adam because she was photocopying documents and getting copies of his records from his health care in Florida and from all the schools he'd attended. Frankly, she was exhausted with the whole process, and the only thing keeping her together was the hope that she could get her son into the residential care he needed. She ran her fingers over the screen and said a silent prayer before closing her computer and falling asleep on the couch.

The ringing of her cell phone three hours later awoke her.

Elena fumbled with the phone and sleepily answered. "Hello?"

"Elena, it's Mary Henderson."

"Hi, Mary." Elena was suddenly wide awake. "How are you today?"

"I'm well, thanks. I wanted to call you before your attorney. We had a meeting today, and I just wanted to tell you that securing funding is looking very good."

"Really?" Elena's eyes widened.

"Yes. Your lawyer fought hard. You should be happy. In fact, I wouldn't be surprised if we get approval as early as next week. Once we do, admission to GLS will be up to the school. I hope they have an opening."

"Oh, that's wonderful news!" Elena's whole body smiled, though she couldn't help a quiver of what-if dread—what if they didn't have an opening? What if all of this was for nothing?

Mary went on. "There will be a requirement that we review his progress every six months to determine whether he is making gains and when he would be ready to return home, but that's not a bad thing."

"No, not at all," Elena said. "It sounds like a way to keep everybody on the same page with what's best for Adam. I'm going to call Carl at GLS and talk with him about Adam's admissions. Thank you so much."

"You're very welcome," Mary said warmly.

CHAPTER 23
ENTHUSIASM

As the elevator doors opened, Elena felt the knot in her stomach loosen just a little at the thought that Adam would be out of Valleyview soon. The cold sterile floors made her lower back hurt just walking from the elevator to his door, and the steady beeping of the heart rate monitor grated on her nerves. She'd never had a problem with hospitals, but knowing that these clean white walls and smell of disinfectant served as her son's drugged-up prison sent a shiver up her spine.

The Phillips family had arrived at Valleyview to pick up Adam and drive him to Oconomowoc.

April, the nurse, smiled as she put her hand on Elena's arm. "I know this isn't where he needed to be for this long, but I'm sure going to miss him."

"Okay. Can we get him?" Shannon was growing anxious at the thought of seeing her brother.

"Of course, go right ahead." April smiled widely. "He certainly is lucky to have such a nice family that cares about him."

"We're the lucky ones, having him," Shannon said as she turned down the hall and led her parents to Adam's room.

"Hey, Squirt!" she exclaimed as she threw open Adam's door. Her childhood nickname for her younger brother was ironic now, as he was almost twice her size.

"Shhh—shhh—!" Adam sat up, flapping his hands in excitement. This was the first time in almost a month that Elena had seen him acting close to himself. His face melted into a smile as he reached for his sister.

"Hey, bubba." Jon walked over to the other side of Adam's bed and put his hands on his son's shoulders. Shannon sat in Adam's lap with her arms around his neck while Elena watched. They were so perfect, almost posed. She reached inside her bag and pulled out her digital camera—she had to have tangible evidence of this moment forever. When the flash erupted in the room, everyone paused. When Adam started to giggle, a collective exhale filled the air.

Loaded in the car, Jon sat behind the steering wheel while his wife and daughter took either side of his son in the backseat. He glanced in the rearview mirror before shifting the car into drive and remembered his sadness the last time he'd experienced this scene. Today, instead of being tearful, Elena and Shannon were joyful. They couldn't contain their excitement at having Adam's personality back and were talking over each other to tell him about his upcoming adventure.

"Now, buddy," Shannon said, "we're not going home. Not yet. We're going to take you to your new school!" Her voice was extra cheerful, because as excited as she was for her brother to have the life he deserved, she missed him terribly and was happy to have him in her arms again. Since he'd been gone, she'd found herself practicing piano late into the night. She was so accustomed to his nocturnal cries that she'd learned to play her key-board with headphones to mute his wailing, but now she played a mourning song to block out the silence of a still house. "Your new school is going to be awesome, but we're going to miss you like crazy, Squirt." Her eyes misted over at the thought of returning home without him yet again.

"Yes, we're going to your school," Elena interjected. "You're going to be with Mr. Will. You will have so much fun. It will make us all very happy."

Shannon regarded her mother. She'd forgotten what she called "Adam-speak," the way that Lyndsey had taught them all to talk to Adam: simple, concrete sentences. Guilt pierced her stomach. How easy it was to let her life with her brother go.

Elena could sense that something was wrong with Shannon, so she reached her hand from around Adam's shoulders to squeeze her daughter. Shannon smiled at the reassurance and turned her attention back to her brother.

"I'm happy you are here," she nuzzled into his neck. "I love you."

Adam giggled in response to his mother and sister leaning into him, while Jon took in the scene from the front seat, his heart swollen with love.

When they arrived at Genesee Lake School, Carl was waiting in the main building.

"This must be Adam." Carl's warm smile contrasted starkly with the snow outside. "It's nice to meet you."

Adam hid behind his mother, his gaze flickering to and away from Carl.

"He's a little shy. It's been a big day," Jon explained.

"That's okay. I thought we'd have him spend some time with Tim, the Vista group supervisor, and then we can meet and talk a bit." Carl helped Jon with a suitcase as he led the way to the same ICARE unit Elena and Jon had visited a month earlier.

Elena and Shannon got Adam's sheets and blankets on the twin bed where he would be sleeping, hung up his posters of The Incredibles and Glee, and started sorting and refolding his clothes into his dresser while Jon sat on the bed with Adam.

"I love you, bubba. I will miss you very much. You will be happy here. I promise. We will come see you." Jon sniffed, trying to hold back his tears. He wasn't sure where they were coming from. Was it a place of sadness that his son wasn't entering his sophomore year of high school, living at home, and raising hell the way he'd done when he was fifteen? Was it a place of relief that Adam was going to get the attention and help that he so richly deserved? Or was it from a place of guilt that he couldn't provide the security that his son and his wife both needed? It didn't matter—he knew he couldn't cry because it would only set Adam off. Jon placed his hands on Adam's shoulders and his nose next to his son's. Elena and Shannon joined them when they had the suitcases unpacked, and they all embraced. Their moment was interrupted by a knock on the door.

"Hi Adam, my name is Will. How are you?" Will's voice rang through the room as he peeked inside.

"Adam, this is Will. He will help you." Elena pulled away from her son so that proper introductions could be made. She thought back to when her six-week maternity leave was up with Adam and she had to leave him with her mother-in-law for the first time. Her heart pounded the same way—her mind raced with "mother bear" thoughts of leaving her young with someone else. Although she trusted Will and this organization, there was a heaviness in her spirit about leaving her baby behind and in the care of others.

"I wanted to introduce you all to Tim. He is the Vista group supervisor. He's a very nice guy."

"Hi, Adam! It's very nice to meet you. I'm Tim. Let's go for a walk and I'll show you our playground area. I heard that you like playgrounds a lot." Tim smiled, and although Adam wasn't looking at him, his shy smile indicated that he liked Tim's voice.

"Let's go, Adam. I'll show you our playground," Tim repeated as he knelt down so that he was eye-to-eye with Adam, who was still sitting on the bed. Adam's eyes lit up at the word playground—even a sedative couldn't temper that enthusiasm.

Tim reached out his hand, which Adam took and stood. His family stood, too, and each hugged Adam before he followed Tim out of the room and to the playground.

The silence behind the closing of Adam's dorm door made their ears ring. They remained silent, trying to process the odd mix of relief, guilt, excitement, and sadness that were simultaneously running through their veins. Jonathan, who sat between his wife and daughter, reached out and wrapped an arm around each of them. He pulled them together as a family of three, feeling Adam's absence more acutely than ever.

Will slowly walked toward the family, sensitive to the range of emotions they were feeling. "This can be tough for families. How are you all doing right now?"

"We're good," Elena replied, sniffling. "It's hard, but for the first time in a while, I think we're good."

"Any time a child leaves the home for a while, there is a period of adjustment. That's normal, and we see it all the time. Would you mind coming to my office to talk more about Adam? I want to get as much information as I can so that we understand his needs as well as possible."

"Not at all," Shannon replied for her parents.

When they returned to Will's office, they all had a seat while he pulled out a notebook.

"I just wanted to follow up on some of the things we discussed last time. Could you tell me some of Adam's strengths?" Will asked.

Shannon, ever her brother's advocate, jumped in first. "He's very loving. He has a great sense of humor, when you can reach him. He's strong and smart."

Elena looked at her daughter in admiration. Shannon had every reason to be angry with or resentful of her brother; instead, she took pride in expounding on his strong points. "Shannon's nailed it, I think," Elena said, looking at Jonathan, who nodded.

"Great! What are some of his interests? What does he like to do? Where does he seem most comfortable?" Will asked.

Elena sat up taller as she spoke. "He likes his iPad. Tight squeezes. Funny faces and tickles. He responded well to his speech and occupational therapy, especially when he was younger. His therapists seemed to enjoy being with him too, because he's lovable and cooperative when the therapy is presented in a playful and fun way. One of his favorite things to do was get a mouthful of spaghetti with Lyndsey and try to make sounds. She knew it was his favorite."

"Thanks, that gives us some good information on how to work with your son. How would you say he relates to or engages with others? How are his social interactions with kids and adults?"

"He's better with adults. Adam doesn't seem very interested in kids except for his sister. It's better if he feels safe and secure, I think." Jon spoke up while he could. "Trust is important to him. It may take him a while to warm up to Tim and the rest of your staff, but once he does, it is easier to get him to follow the routine. There are certainly times when he just wants to do his own thing, but when he trusts you, it's easier to get him to switch gears."

"Great, thanks a lot. Tell me about daily living skills. How about using the bathroom?" asked Will.

"He's fully toilet trained and needs no assistance. I do check once in a while just to make sure," Elena said with a mother's pride.

"How about brushing his teeth?" Will asked.

"He'll do it, but he needs some help to do it properly," Elena continued. "I have to give him some verbal reminders, and we keep the toothbrush and toothpaste out for him."

"What about showering?"

"Pretty much on his own. I do smell his hair to make sure he shampooed. He loves baths, but showers are good."

"How about mealtimes and eating?"

"Like we told you before, he is a picky eater," Elena explained, "but he does fine with feeding himself. He might need some reminders to wipe his face, but it's okay overall. He's able to bring dishes to the sink when he's finished."

"Does he dress himself?"

"I put his clothes out for him in the morning, but he gets dressed on his own. He wears Uggs or slides because he has trouble with shoelaces, and he sometimes needs help zipping his heavy coat. He doesn't like button-top jeans and has trouble with the zipper. We have packed mostly elastic waist pants, because he is most comfortable in those. Basically, he needs someone to pick out his clothes for him, and he does the rest."

"How does he sleep at night?"

"Not very well right now. I think it's the Abilify. He used to take something in the past to help with sleep, but I can't remember the name. He can have a hard time falling asleep, and he wakes up early a few times a week."

"Any significant medical or dental concerns I should pass on to health services?"

"No. Physically, he's a very healthy boy."

"Thanks. This has been very helpful. Families are very important, and we do everything we can to make sure they are involved in a child's care. Could you tell me about your family? What do you see as your strengths?"

They all looked at one another. The idea of them as a family, or a team, had not been something they had thought about in a while because all of the focus was always on Adam and his needs.

"We're funny," Shannon said, looking between her parents uncertainly.

"We love each other very much," Jon said.

"We do whatever it takes," Elena added.

"Thanks. It can be a real struggle for families when a child receives out-of-home care," Will said. "How do you make sense out of Adam attending GLS?"

"He needs to be here, because I can't do what's best for him at home, and I refuse to let my son rot in a hospital. You can teach him the skills that he needs, help him communicate and regulate himself better, and maybe he'll even learn how to make a friend. I hope that you can also keep him happy and that he can have the best life possible," Elena said passionately. "Shannon has a full music scholarship to Northwestern University that will start this fall. Adam will never accomplish what Shannon does in school, but I want him to be equally ful-filled and pleased with his own accomplishments—they will just be different." Elena's pulse raced. She couldn't believe she'd just been that open with Will. These were the thoughts and hopes she kept to herself for fear they'd sound silly. She saw Shannon wiping away tears and felt Jon giving her knee an encouraging squeeze.

"I'd like to say something, Will," Jon said. "Back to the strengths of our family. It's Elena. She is the strength of our family. She's kept us together and found the courage to do what's best for Adam. She's an amazing mother, and I couldn't ask for a better wife." His voice broke.

"Thanks," Will said softly, making notes. He cleared his throat as the moment washed between husband and wife.

"Wow, thanks Jon." Elena blushed a little.

"It's wonderful to see you all so joined, despite the difficulties that you've overcome and those that may lie ahead." Will cleared his throat. "How often are you plan-ning to visit?"

"I'd come every day, but I know that's just not possible," Elena replied. "But can I call?"

"Of course. Many of our parents call every night, and even if their kids aren't able to talk on the phone, they can speak with me or one of our staff for an update. I also communicate with many of our parents on a weekly basis by email, if you would like that."

"That's excellent," Elena said, nodding at Jonathan. "And as for visiting, we'd like to come most weekends. Of course, it won't always be all three of us, but we're going to do the best we can to take mini-vacations together here."

"We would ask that your first visit be on-grounds in two weeks, then gradually off-grounds in the community," Will said.

"Two weeks . . ." Elena trailed off. She'd never been away from her son that long. She bit her lip. "Okay. Well, I know it's only March, but what about holidays?"

"It really depends on Adam's adjustment and progress and will be a constant discussion point during our phone calls," Will said. "Home visits also depend on how you are feeling about your ability to support him there at that time."

Elena nodded. *At least Christmas at home is an option,* she thought, trying to stay optimistic.

"I'll give you a call tomorrow, but feel free to call me if you have any questions," Will said, "Our staff will get to know Adam better over the next few weeks, and we'll need more input from you, of course."

"Of course. We'll tell you whatever you need to help our son," Jon said.

"Do you have any other questions?" Will asked.

Jon and Elena looked at each other. "No," Elena said. "I think we're good. I would ask if we could go see Adam once more, but I think that it would be harder for all of us to say goodbye again."

"He's in good hands, Laney." Jon put his hand on the small of Elena's back as they rose from their chairs.

"You're right," Elena said, resigned. "Let's go."

In the car, Jon surprised everyone when he turned to Shannon in the backseat.

"Give me your iPod."

"What?" Shannon looked shocked.

"We're listening to your music now." His eyes were stinging with tears, and he was trying to distract himself from the weight on his chest. The grief was raw—his stomach felt as if it had been rubbed with sandpaper—and he just needed the silence of people and the bang of drums, the crash of symbols, and the steady thump of a good bass line.

Shannon hooked up her iPod to the stereo, and Jon and Elena listened to their daughter's favorite songs, many of which were songs they had enjoyed when they were young and had no idea their daughter even knew about—much less loved. When Barenaked Ladies' "What a Good Boy" flowed through their stereo, silent tears ran down everyone's cheeks.

"Let's go out to dinner," Jon said impulsively when they hit the Madison city limits.

"Really?" Elena asked.

"Yes. I went to this amazing little Italian place for lunch the other day, and—"

"Is it Romeo's?" Shannon exclaimed from the backseat.

"It is, actually." Jon was surprised.

"I love it there! We've gone after rehearsal sometimes. It's great."

"Well, Elena, looks like you're the only one who—"

"I've been there, too," Elena said, laughing. "It's next to my salon, and I've grabbed a slice of pizza on my way home. So, I guess we've all experienced the brilliance that is Romeo's."

"But not together," Jon smiled. "Let's do it."

The restaurant was cozy, with terra cotta floors and old, framed pictures of Frank Sinatra on the wall. In the background, Old Blue Eyes crooned that the best was yet to come. Elena took that as a sign.

"Buongiorno!" They were greeted by a small old man. "I am Giancarlo, and I'm so happy that you are here. Come! Have a seat! Would you like some wine?"

Elena felt as though she were family already as they followed the old man to their table. She and Jon ordered a bottle of cabernet sauvignon, and Shannon asked for a cherry Coke. While Giancarlo went to place their drink orders, the family scanned the menu.

"I'm Gina, Giancarlo's daughter." A young girl with long, wavy dark hair and wearing a "Romeo's" shirt walked up and stood by the table. She set two empty glasses in front of Elena and Jon and the bottle of wine between them. She then placed Shannon's cherry Coke before her. Finally, she drew a basket of bread from where she'd balanced it in the crook of her elbow and set it before them. "Dad loves his restaurant and his guests, if you couldn't tell."

Elena smiled. "We love it. I've grabbed a slice of pizza to go, but I haven't been able to eat here yet."

"Well, you're in for a treat. My mother is the head chef.

She's fabulous." Gina patted her non-existent tummy. "I'm just lucky that I got my dad's genes. Do you have any questions about the menu?"

"Actually, I do. I don't see chicken tenders on here. Can you make those?" Elena asked.

"Umm . . . I'm sure that we could make those," Gina said, looking surprised.

"Mom, are you really going to come to this awesome Italian place and eat fried chicken?" Shannon asked.

"Well, they're for . . ." Elena's voice trailed off. She was looking to order for Adam. Although they didn't venture out to eat with him, she often ordered chicken tenders to go so that he could have them later. Everyone at the table realized what she'd done and became misty eyed. "Never mind, Gina," Elena almost whispered. "Can we start with an antipasto platter?"

"Yum!" Jonathan's voice broke his tears.

When Gina went to put in the orders, Jon turned to his daughter. "Tell us everything, Shan. What's new in your world?" His heart was racing. He realized that he'd never been able to devote the attention to Shannon that she deserved. He didn't want her to feel he was prying or overacting in a too-little-too-late way.

"Nothing. Everything is about the same." Shannon tore the crusts off her bread and dipped them into the olive oil on her plate. She was surprised. Her father had never asked her about her life—and certainly not in the light, gossipy tone that he was employing tonight. She was a little skeptical of his question, but her deeply buried resentment loosened a bit in her chest. She couldn't help feeling a warm glow at the attention from her parents.

"Exactly the same?" Elena asked teasingly, relieved

that her daughter was conversational.

"Well, school is fine. My GPA is consistent with what it has been. I love my senior music seminars. I'm starting to compose some fun stuff. Of course, it's just for fun, but I'm enjoying it. I'm just hanging out with my friends and making music. Getting ready for the prom. Living the dream," Shannon chuckled.

"That all sounds good. And generic. Give us some dirt. Come on. We're your parents." Elena poked her daughter's ribs.

"Well, there is someone . . . special," Shannon ventured, color rising to her cheeks. "He's asked if he can be my prom date."

"Oh!" Elena said, looking at Jonathan. This was the first time Shannon had expressed real interest in a boy. "That's wonderful! What's his name?"

"William. He's a cellist. He's really funny. We're going to prom together, but in a group. It should be fun. Not too much pressure," Shannon was quick to add, avoiding her father's eyes. Although she was a senior in high school, she'd always been so devoted to her music and her studies that she hadn't ever had a serious boyfriend. She'd dated here and there, but she didn't go out much for fear of leaving her mother alone with Adam.

"William, eh?" Jon asked, trying unsuccessfully to keep his voice light. "Did you tell him that we're from the south?"

"Oh, Daddy." Shannon rolled her eyes. "It's not like that."

"Yeah, it better not be. I'd hate to have to call Northwestern and cancel your enrollment because I've locked you in your room forever." Jon was teasing his daughter, but his face quickly fell when he saw his wife and daughter avert their eyes to their laps. The meal struck a somber tone. Elena sipped her wine and Gina brought the appetizer platter, which they ate quietly until their meals came and their conversation resumed.

CHAPTER 24
YOU ARE IN CLASS

"Adam, Ms. Georgia is your teacher," Will told Adam as he walked him into the classroom. "This is your classroom." He guided the young man into the classroom and helped him take a seat on one of the comfortable seats arranged in a circle. The small desks in front of the padded chairs each held a file folder with the individual student's photograph and name printed across the front. There were three other students with three ICARE staff in the classroom; their folders read Vivian, Tucker, and James. The walls were a light grey, with lamps set up instead of the bright, overhead fluorescent lights typically found in a classroom. On the right wall, opposite the row of windows, was artwork made by the class the week before.

"Hi, Adam. It's nice to meet you." Georgia walked over to Adam sitting in the plush seat. "Could you come with me?" she asked, making a gesture with her hand that he should follow. Georgia was a certified special education teacher and had worked with mostly nonverbal students with autism for the better part of ten years. Her experience and intuition told her that despite Adam's size, the sweetest heart lay within his chest. She pulled back her shoulders, which accentuated her height, tucked her long blond hair behind her ears, and adjusted her glasses once she was close to him.

Adam looked down, but he followed Georgia to the wall, where the classroom visual schedule was displayed. On the wall were sixteen squares of paper, each with a simple word and picture to demonstrate the activity planned. "Look here, Adam. This tells us when things happen and what happens next." Georgia smiled at Adam. "First we get our folders, which are here, and then we will work on art." She motioned to the pictures of the folder and the art supplies.

Adam patted his belly. He'd eaten a good breakfast that morning, ripping up the doughy circles of his pancakes and dipping them into maple syrup. He giggled as the sticky concoction slid across his plate and onto the pieces of bread. He pulled them into his mouth greedily. The memory made him lift his hands to his mouth.

"It's not time to eat yet. Let's look at your folder." Georgia sat Adam down with his folder. "Your picture is here, and your name is here: Adam Phillips." She'd written his name across the folder in big, bold letters with a Sharpie. "Your papers go in here." She placed a box of Crayola washable markers before him, along with a piece of poster board she'd cut into quarters. Georgia walked to the board, where she'd drawn a rudimentary house: a triangle on top of a rectangle. She filled in windows and doors and turned back to the class. "This is my house. I leave my house to visit my friends at GLS: Vivian, Tucker, James, and Adam. You left your house to visit us, too. Draw your house for me."

Adam loved to draw, and he especially loved markers.

When he was at the day school, he was frustrated that some of the other students in his class could use markers while he had a box of fat crayons. Crayons never stayed sharp enough to make the skinny lines that Adam saw in his mind and couldn't translate to the page. He began flapping his arms with excitement before he picked up the yellow cardboard box. In his haste to get to drawing, he ripped the box. Markers clattered onto his desk, where they rolled off and to the floor.

"Gaaaah!" Adam exclaimed in frustration. The eight markers went in eight different directions. He couldn't reach them all at once, and he wanted to use them so badly. He finally had markers, and now they were all over the floor, and he couldn't get them. He rose quickly to collect them, but yellow and green were underfoot and rolled, causing him to fall on the floor. Slam. He hit the tile before Tim could get over to him, and already on the floor, he started to wail and hit the floor with his hand as hard as he could. Tim got behind him on the floor and, remembering what Elena and Jon said about deep pressure, pulled Adam's shoulders together in an embrace. He felt the young man's shoulders begin to relax, and the hand pounding ceased. After a few seconds, Adam's whole body released and his breathing started to calm. Georgia walked over to Adam. "Let's pick up those markers so we can draw," she said cheerfully. "Adam, draw a picture of your house."

Adam crawled back up into his seat and grasped the purple marker as tightly as his hand could. He soon filled the white paper with streaks of purple grass upon which his orange house would sit.

CHAPTER 25
SIMPLE SOLUTIONS

"So, his first day was good?" Elena asked Will over the phone. She'd had knots in her stomach all day. She was worried that Genesee Lake School was too good to be true—that they wouldn't be able to handle Adam and they'd call her to pick him up.

"He did well," Will said. "He had a couple of rough moments, during art and during lunch. Like I said, though, when he became agitated and unregulated, we were able to prevent escalation, and he calmed down pretty quickly. Our OT ordered a weighted blanked that arrives tomorrow, which will be a part of his sensory diet here at GLS."

"Weighted blanket?" Elena shifted in her seat at her kitchen table.

"Yes. When you told Carl that you and Jon hold Adam until he calms, our occupational therapist reviewed his IEP and OT records and realized that he might benefit from deep pressure for sensory regulation. Many children and adolescents struggle with regulating their sensory system. We can order the blankets or we have a seamstress on staff who makes them. The blanket will be about ten percent of his body weight, and he will have a schedule developed by our occupational therapist so that Adam can use it in school and in the living area."

"That sounds like a wonderful idea. Please let me know if it works so that we can try it at home." Elena was truly amazed at how this simple thing might help.

"A big part of our job is to figure out tools that help kids, then make sure that parents and school districts know what works for the child—so yes, of course, we'll let you know," Will said, and Elena could hear the smile in his voice.

"Thank you so much for checking in with me. I know that it's almost time for you to go home, but I appreciate you taking the time to talk."

"We'll do it every day if we need to." Again, Will's voice was warm and reassuring. "Adam is a great kid, and he's doing very well. Thank you for trusting us with him."

"Thank you for taking such good care of him when we can't. Goodbye now. We'll talk tomorrow."

Elena pushed the END button on her cell phone and fell back into her seat with a deep breath. Although Jon had to work late that night, she knew that he would be excited to hear the update when he got home. She could only imagine that he was as nervous as she had been about Adam's first day.

To keep her mind off things, she spent part of the afternoon looking online for jobs. If things worked out at GLS, there was no reason she couldn't go back to work. They could maybe get a handle on the credit card debt they'd accumulated over the past ten years, and she could actually get out of the house once in a while. Most importantly, she could begin rebuilding her career. She had a passion for working sales, and the district manager job that was open at another store was enticing. Without thinking, she put together a resume and sent off a letter of intent. She was certainly qualified, and while retail jobs often meant weekends, a district manager worked mostly weekdays. Shannon would be away at college in just a few months, and Elena could make the travel requirements work.

The chime on her home alarm beeped, indicating that Jon was home from work. He set down his lunchbox in the kitchen and made his way to the table where Elena was sitting.

"Hey, sweetheart," he said, kissing his wife on the cheek. "How are you doing?"

"I'm actually great," Elena replied, her voice more up-beat than it had been in a while. "I spoke with Will, and Adam did really well today."

"That's wonderful," Jon smiled, "I'm relieved to hear that."

"Me, too. I was a nervous wreck until he called."

"I've been pretty preoccupied myself," Jon admitted. "You know, in the back of my mind, I thought I would be relieved when Adam was away, but I think about him just as much now, if not more."

"I know. I can't believe it will be two weeks until we get to see him. I understand, though, that it's for the best." Elena's eyes stung with tears. Even though he hadn't been home in a month, she was used to visiting him at Valleyview every day.

Jon reached across the table to find his wife's hand. "It's all going to be okay. Will said you could call every day. This is better for all of us. I'm proud of you, Laney. You've been able to let go and let others help."

CHAPTER 26
MR. INCREDIBLE

The next morning, Tim came into Adam's room after breakfast to help him get ready for his day.

"Good morning, Adam. It's time to make your bed!" Tim's voice was enthusiastic, attempting to engage Adam in a shared experience of daily living skills.

Adam looked briefly at Tim, which was an improvement over the previous day when he'd barely acknowledged Tim's presence.

"We're going to start with the white sheet. Where is the white sheet?" Tim pointed to the pile of sheets that he'd put on Adam's bed.

Adam pointed to the white sheet. "Great job!" Tim exclaimed. "Put it on your bed." Tim used hand motions and gestures to demonstrate how to lay the sheet flat and smooth it over the bed. Adam looked around, obviously trying to avoid Tim, so he grabbed the sheet and knotted it around his neck. "Adam, do you like Mr. Incredible? Look! I'm Mr. Incredible!" Adam looked up and giggled as Tim put up his arm as though he were flying. "We must make bed before the evil robots destroy it!"

Adam was giggling but got up and stood beside Tim,

who untied the sheet and put it in Adam's hands. He put his hands over the young boy's, guiding them as they smoothed and tucked the sheet into the corners.

"We did it!" Tim exclaimed. "Great job!" He held up his hand to Adam, who responded with a high five. Adam looked at Tim and smiled.

Back in Madison, Elena took on her new fitness resolution—Jillian Michael's Thirty-Day Shred. She had just collapsed onto her couch with her water bottle when her cell phone rang. Her stomach tied up in knots when she realized that she didn't recognize the number on her caller ID.

"Hello?" She was breathless, her voice small from the anxiety rising in her chest.

"Elena? Hi! This is Stephanie Rogers, the regional manager for Gap Incorporated. How are you today?"

"I'm fine, thank you. How are you?" Relief and surprise washed over Elena. Not only was the call not GLS asking her to pick up Adam as she'd feared, but it was a call back from the first resume she'd sent out in the better part of ten years.

"I'm great, thanks. So, I got your resume, and I know it's not a lot of notice, but would you be free to meet at the Banana Republic at Riverdale tomorrow? It's the one closest to your house, and I'll be there for the morning. I'm spending the rest of the week in Milwaukee, and I'd like to get to know you better before I go."

"I—sure," Elena said, flustered and excited. "I'd love to meet you. That would be great. What time?"

"Let's say ten a.m.? I'll meet you at the store, and then maybe we can go to Starbucks and grab a coffee. I have hard copies of everything you sent over, so no need to bring anything except your smile."

The sweetly cheesy line made Elena grin. "That sounds great, Stephanie. Thanks so much." Despite her sore legs, Elena practically danced as she hung up the phone. She had a job interview—a promising one at that.

CHAPTER 27
CONCENTRATION

"Here is your medication. Make sure you also drink some water." Tim gave Adam his prescribed amount of Abilify—now half of his previous dose. Dr. Refel, the consulting GLS psychiatrist, thought that Adam would be less sedated, get more restful sleep, and lose weight without as much of the medication, so he had started a gradual reduction of the Abilify. Will and the ICARE staff monitored his behavior and communicated any concerns to Dr. Refel directly.

Tim walked Adam to his classroom, where Georgia was waiting with the other students. Adam collected his folder and waited for directions from his teacher. Georgia handed out black construction paper and colored chalk to the students.

"Vivian, Adam, Tucker, and James are my friends. I like my friends," Georgia told the class after she'd distributed all the supplies. "But I have a family that I love, too. I have a mommy and a daddy, a husband, and a daughter. You are a son or daughter, too. Today we will draw pictures of our family. All the people in your family."

Adam stuck out his tongue with concentration. He

was going to draw his mother and father and Shannon. He missed them. Mommy was warm and soft, so she would be orange. Daddy was strong and funny, so he would be yellow. And Shannon was beautiful and kind, so she would be green and blue—like the sky he tried to reach on the swing. After five minutes of furious drawing, he had completed his picture. Will sat next to him and admired the three stick figures, rudimentary but each drawn with such care. "Your family drawing is very good," he said, leaning over to Adam.

Adam, who normally looked down at his drawing when Will spoke, looked up into his coordinator's brown eyes. Adam's own brown eyes grew wide, and a smile played at his mouth. He started to giggle and leaned into Will, putting his head on his chest for just a second before moving his attention back to Georgia, who'd started to speak again.

CHAPTER 28
NEW RITUALS

"I'm just so proud of you, Mom. It takes a lot to go after a job when you haven't worked in so long. But you got it!" Shannon was exuberant in the backseat. The family was on their way out for a celebratory dinner.

"Thank you, darling. I'm still in a bit of shock myself." Elena smiled back at her daughter.

"I knew you could do it, Laney." Jon reached over and squeezed Elena's knee.

"I think what surprised me the most was Stephanie's willingness to work with my weekends. She understood that Adam is a priority and that I'd like to visit him each weekend. Only a few will be a problem, and I'll still be able to have the time off for our vacation celebrating Shannon's graduation. It's just perfect. I'm so happy." Elena was beaming. Not only was she offered the perfect job, but also her baby was doing well at his new school. She'd been talking with Will briefly each day, and Adam's transition to GLS had gone better than she ever expected. Her heart was exploding with gratitude as they pulled into the parking lot of Romeo's. Since their dinner there after dropping Adam off at GLS two weeks ago, it had become their place, and they were trying to make a weekly ritual of visiting.

"I miss Adam," Shannon blurted while they tucked into their antipasto platter. "It's just so weird that he isn't at home."

"I know," Jon said. He opened his mouth to elaborate but realized that he couldn't find words to express his simultaneous sadness and relief, accompanied by a pang of guilt in his stomach.

"What's so hard is that I miss him so much, but I'm so excited about my new job," Elena said, her eyes filling with tears. "I know that wouldn't have happened if Adam were still living with us, and I know that he's where he needs to be, but I'm having trouble balancing these emotions."

"Yes!" Shannon exclaimed. "I know exactly what you mean. I'm thrilled that I get to have both of you at my senior recital. That I can go out with my friends and not worry about being home as soon as possible. But I'm having a tough time enjoying myself because I should feel worse about Adam not being at home. It's like I'm in total conflict with myself and I can't figure it out."

Elena slipped her arm around her daughter's shoulders. "Well, we'll go see him in a couple weeks. It will all be worth it. I promise." Her reassurance came despite her own questions about the situation. That truth was that Elena still woke up to Adam's phantom cries in the night. Whenever she started the car after forgetting to lower the car radio volume after a previous drive, she winced and glanced in her rearview mirror, waiting for Adam's meltdown to begin. She thought back to after she had Shannon, when she visited her OB-GYN for her six-week appointment, exhausted and overwhelmed with the care of her new baby. The doctor had smiled and told her that she would adjust to her new normal in a few months, and by that time, Shannon wouldn't be a tiny baby anymore. Elena comforted herself, knowing that she'd gotten used to so much before and that there were bright possibilities ahead for the whole family.

CHAPTER 29
OUT OF THE MOUTHS OF BABES

"Squirt!" Shannon exclaimed as she rushed into his dorm room. "We're so happy to see you!"

Adam looked to the door when he heard his sister's voice. He looked up from his iPad, and when he saw Shannon come towards him, he stood and let her hug him. When she let go, he saw Jon and Elena standing close to the door. He grinned at his parents.

Elena let the tears roll down her cheeks. She hadn't seen him look this well in a long time. She thought back to the last time she'd seen him, exactly two weeks ago. He was much more alert than he'd been in the hospital, and he seemed content. He took Shannon's hand and led her to his bed, where he showed her the app he'd been playing with on his iPad. It was a memory game of sorts, where he would match a word to a picture. He played the game in school during his time in the computer lab and liked it so much that Will put it on the iPad. He showed Shannon the brown horse and then scrolled through the words until the bottom of the screen said HORSE. When he clicked on the screen to make a match, the horse made a neighing sound, and Adam giggled and clapped his hands.

"You can do it, buddy! I'm so proud of you!" Shannon wrapped her arm around her brother's waist. Adam giggled and quickly went about finding the word BIRD so that he could make the robin on his iPad sing. Will and Dr. Mike, the GLS psychologist, came into Adam's room after the family had time to greet each other.

"Mr. and Mrs. Phillips? Shannon? Hi, I'm Dr. Mike, the GLS psychologist. It's very nice to meet you. Will told me you were coming, and I just wanted to pop in and say hi." He extended a hand to each of the family members and asked if he could speak with Elena and Jon alone.

"Sure," Jon said, following Dr. Mike to his office.

When they were seated, Dr. Mike pulled out a file.

"As you can see, Adam is doing very well and settling in nicely. Will and the ICARE staff have been reporting that he's doing well in both school and the group living areas. As you know, our psychiatrist has also gradually reduced the amount of Abilify. It sounds like he came to us on a pretty high dose. We're not finding any significant side effects to this point."

"That's great to hear," said Elena, infused with relief.

"Our initial evaluation process typically takes a few weeks to complete, as we want to make sure that each child is acclimated to GLS before we develop an individual treatment plan. We do a number of things, such as identifying a child's interests, comfort zone activities, and capacities for attention and regulation, engagement and relating, two-way communication, and more complex problem solving. Adam really enjoys artwork and recess, so we use those activities to build upon the developmental levels that we discussed before. Remember, in the DIR model, it's never too late to strengthen developmental foundations in relating, communicating, and thinking."

"It makes a lot of sense that you use his interests to kind of get into his world so that you can strengthen those skills," Jon replied.

"It does, yes, and emotion is key—so doing things that he enjoys and finds meaningful in the context of a helping relationship, with us using affect and emotion as well, are the vehicles of change," said Dr. Mike. "I wanted to ask about your family. So, how are you doing?" Dr. Mike's brown eyes crinkled in the corners as he offered an understanding smile.

"We're doing just great. I started working a couple weeks ago. I haven't worked in so long that I'm still a little nervous, but more excited," Elena gushed. "Shannon is still doing well in school, preparing for graduation. Jon is still working hard as ever."

"That sounds really good, Elena. Everybody else in the family feel the same way?" Dr. Mike could see that Elena was giving him a superficial overview of their home life.

"We miss Adam, I'll be honest." Shannon piped in. "We're keeping busy and doing well, but none of us quite know what to do with ourselves after dinner. It's weird. It's hard to come to terms with what we all went through, what is happening now, and what the future holds."

Out of the mouths of babes, Elena thought, putting her hand on her daughter's knee and giving Dr. Mike a small nod. The past, present, and future.

"As a family, you're going through a period of adjustment. Maybe it's your first time to really think and not react. This is a big change for you. You've dealt with the challenges of caring for a child with very significant special needs for a long time, and it takes a toll—on individuals and relationships. For many families, it takes time and support to come out the other side. Some families find counseling helpful. It's important that, as Adam learns and grows as a person, your family be allowed to do the same. Do you have any thoughts on family counseling?"

Dr. Mike's words struck a chord with Elena. While she'd suspected in the back of her mind that her family should have some therapy—a place to hash everything out with one another and for themselves—she was afraid that going would be admitting they couldn't handle it all on their own. Sending Adam to Genesee Lake School had also been an example of that, but it was justified through the tools and professional training that the school could offer Adam. Family counseling, meanwhile, meant that they couldn't hold themselves together. There was something almost humiliating about the thought. Still . . .

"Well, my new health insurance has mental health coverage," Elena offered. "It's certainly something that we will look into." She smiled at the psychologist.

"Sometimes it helps to have a neutral person, someone outside the family, guide the discussion. Plus, trust me," Dr. Mike said with a laugh, "there's no lifetime commitment. You could just try it and see how it goes. It might help. I've seen it help before."

Jon shifted in his seat. He could tell Elena wasn't entirely sold on the prospect, but the fact that she knew about her insurance coverage indicated that she'd already explored the idea. He didn't need to go to a head shrinker. They were for crazy people, or people with severe disabilities. People like Adam needed psychologists and therapists. He fought the urge to roll his eyes at his wife's compliance. He knew full well, though, that she wouldn't let the idea go now that it was in her head.

While Adam's family was meeting with Dr. Mike and Will, Shannon was able to observe Adam's Floortime. After school each day, Margaret, one of the ICARE staff, worked with Adam either individually or paired with another child. Today, it was just Adam. He had chosen to finger paint, so Margaret took his lead and grabbed some art supplies. She explained to Shannon that her overall goal was to harness Adam's natural interests, like finger painting, in order to build upon developmental capacities associated with attention and regulation, engagement and relating, purposeful communication, and shared problem solving. Shannon nodded, surprised at the nice table Margaret had set up. She had the three primary colors in glass jars placed on one side of the table, along with cards that said MORE, ENOUGH, and ALL DONE.

Shannon stood in the corner as Margaret led Adam to the table.

"Great, Adam, you want to finger paint," Margaret said cheerily. "What color would you like?"

Adam's hands flapped excitedly. He ran his hands over the white paper before him. It was smooth and clean. He longed to fill it with color and gestured to all the paint.

"Hmm . . . I'm confused," Margaret said with a frown, holding out her hands. It was slightly dramatic, as though she were acting in a play. "Tell me the color, Adam. What color do you want?" Margaret's voice became more cheerful.

Adam pondered the choices before pointing to yellow.

"Thank you for showing me what color you want! Here you go, Adam." She opened the little jar and let Adam stick his finger in before taking it away.

He looked at her, confused and a bit angry.

"Do you want more? Show me MORE?" Margaret asked, pointing at the card that read such.

"More!" Adam exclaimed, pointing to the MORE sign.

Margaret immediately opened the jar and placed it in front of him. "Nice job telling me 'more,' Adam. That was awesome!"

Shannon was amazed at Margaret's ability to engage her brother yet also push him to interact, communicate, and problem solve—maybe not clearly with words, but with gestures. She couldn't believe the progress he'd made in just a couple weeks. The ICARE staff had said it was not unusual for kids to benefit rapidly from the structure, routine, consistency, and staff understanding of autism and underdeveloped skills, but Shannon was still stunned. She had seen her mother try to make him smile during fun activities like this, while Margaret—a twenty-one-year-old social work college student and GLS direct care professional—seemed to intuitively know how to use her own affect and Adam's interests to enter his world and practice relating, communicating, and thinking. And all through having fun? It seemed so natural, easy, kid-like, and real to Shannon—unlike anything she had ever seen or thought about before. And it was working for Adam.

CHAPTER 30
NORMAL

"I guess I just saw what Elena and Shannon were doing, and I wanted to be a part of it. I wanted to participate with them," Jon said as he shifted in his chair. It had been six weeks since their first weekend visit with Adam, when Dr. Mike had brought up therapy for the family. Elena and Shannon had gone once a week, and they usually came home laughing despite their red eyes and tear-stained cheeks.

At first, Jon thought the whole idea was stupid. He was grateful that Elena was making money and that her insurance was covering the therapy—but thought that therapy itself was just an excuse for women to sit around and cry. Last week, though, he'd noticed something different. When Elena was cooking dinner, Shannon came into the kitchen to help. Shannon was always dutiful—the child who loaded the dishwasher and put away her laundry (and sometimes theirs) without being asked. However, for years she'd sat in front of her piano or with a book in her room unless she was expected to be with the family. That day, though, Shannon came into the kitchen to be with Elena on her own. She and her mother were working on a new recipe for eggplant Parmesan that Shannon had found online. The two women were bobbing their heads in time with Fiona Apple's "Not About Love" as they measured and tasted.

"This is the part!" Shannon exclaimed. The songstress's voice slowly dragged out how she missed a stupid ape before the music became strangely syncopated and she ran lyrics through her tongue in almost a rap. Jon didn't understand why anyone would like that discordant noise and looked to Elena to share a smile about their age when he noticed that she was just as into it as her daughter.

"You're so right, Shan!" Elena caught her breath as the music subsided. "That was just like a tantrum. They were pretty intense, weren't they?" She took a step back, mentally, to admire her daughter. "It's so neat that you can place that feeling with music. You're so talented." Elena reached over to her daughter and embraced her, fully. Both women held each other for a pregnant moment, reveling in their closeness.

Now, two weeks later, Jonathan sat with Elena and Shannon in Dr. Barron's richly appointed office. She was a young psychologist who had taken over her father's practice when he retired. Seeing the Phillips family was one of her favorite times of the week. They cared very much about each other and had experienced a great deal of trauma that they hadn't dealt with for years. "How have you been since Adam's been at GLS?"

"Great," Jon said. "The house is quiet, and we're all getting along."

"Really?" Dr. Barron raised an eyebrow.

"That's just it. Everything is wonderful and I feel so horribly guilty that his absence feels this good. We're a family of four. We should mourn the loss of him. And I do, I miss him terribly, but it's really nice to come home from work and find my wife and daughter cooking dinner. It's nice not to wince every time my cell phone rings while I'm at work. It's nice to feel normal." Jonathan's voice cracked. He hadn't expected to "go there" in his first session. But when he started talking, he realized how much there was inside him just bursting to get out. Shannon caught her father's eye, and when he looked up and saw tears falling from her eyes, he felt his heart click into place with hers.

CHAPTER 31
HOPE

"Welcome to the recital, Mr. and Mrs. Phillips," Joy Garrison, Shannon's piano teacher throughout her high school career, greeted Jon and Elena in the lobby of the theatre. She handed them a program. "Shannon is our final pianist tonight—a place of honor. I know that she makes you as proud as she makes me."

"She's really wonderful," Elena agreed, beaming and grateful for the teacher's dedication to Shannon. "I can't believe she's graduating from high school this weekend."

"Only three more days!" Joy exclaimed. "Will Adam make it to the ceremony?"

"He won't, sadly," Elena said. "We're afraid that the crowd would be too much for him. We're going to get him for a weekend visit as soon as we get back from Canada, though. We'll celebrate as a family."

"That sounds lovely. Listen, I have to run backstage, but enjoy!" Joy hurried through the double doors into the theatre as Jon and Elena found their seats. After they settled in, Elena flipped through the program's heavy paper. The thick ink upon brilliant white glossy pages struck her as almost unbearably beautiful. Shannon's name was scrolled beside a print of her senior picture. Her blond hair fell in waves down her shoulders onto the requisite black velvet wrap, green eyes piercing over her full lips that fell into the half smirk that Shannon wore most of the time. The words Honored Pianist were written beside her name. Elena's heart swelled. Her daughter had placed above all the other musicians she had studied with for the past four years. Over the next few minutes, Elena scanned the autobiographical information about Shannon: her GPA, her plans to attend Northwestern on a full scholarship . . . but she stopped short when she saw the last line of her daughter's brief history. "Miss Phillips thanks her parents, Jon and Elena, for always encouraging and inspiring her. Most of all, she thanks her brother, Adam, who couldn't be here tonight but who lives each day in unbridled emotion and taught her to move with the music in her heart." Elena gasped as tears filled her eyes. She handed the program over to Jon and took his hand. The houselights dimmed as the concert began.

After applauding the twelve other concert pianists, it was finally time for Shannon to take the stage. The spotlight fell on the grand piano in the center of the stage, and Shannon's black, floor-length dress camouflaged her with the darkness until she took her seat at the bench. Once the applause died down, Shannon's fingers paused tentatively over the keys. She took a deep breath and slowly began to coax Beethoven's Moonlight Sonata from the keys. Each finger stroke was deliberate, and the melancholic tones filled the theatre. The song was one of hopes unrealized, longing in its intention, and Elena saw their journey—everything she'd wanted for both her children, the dreams for her family, all that happened and didn't happen . . . Shannon's grace and poise on the piano bench moved Elena to tears. As she wiped her eyes, she realized she was crying because Shannon had grown up so perfect not despite her situation but because of it. Perfection was Shannon's hard-fought way of coping. She was so strong and graceful and talented. In that moment, Elena wasn't sure she deserved her daughter.

Jon held his wife's hand and didn't realize until the third movement, when the music picked up, that he'd been holding his breath. His chest swelled, his heart beating in his ears at the thought of his daughter's ability to take something so desperate and transform it into something unimaginably beautiful. In the repetition of the flowing melody, he could feel her sadness and sense the holding pattern in which Shannon had spent her young life. Then, as it opened up at the end, something else emerged: his daughter's delicate, unvarnished hope.

CHAPTER 32
A NEW ROUTINE

"We won't be able to visit next week, as we'll be in Canada. I just wanted to make sure that you remembered," Elena said to Will on her cell phone. She was getting everything ready for their trip and wanted to check in with Will once more before they left.

"I know, Elena. Don't worry about it. Adam is doing great, and he will be excited to see you all when you get back. You're still taking him for the weekend in two weeks, right?"

"Yes! We can't wait to have him back. Shannon has to go to Illinois in six weeks, so we want to have as much family time with him as possible. Please give my sweet boy kisses and hugs from us all."

"I will, thanks for checking in. Have a fun trip, and don't worry about anything down here."

Will hung up the phone and smiled before heading upstairs to see how the group was doing.

In the classroom, Georgia had a surprise for Adam. She'd noticed during art that Adam had a particular affinity for the foam rubber shapes that they were pasting to their paper, so she had created a foam rubber alphabet and numbers for Adam to use during reading and math time. After ten minutes of the skin brushing part of his sensory diet, during which his occupational therapist pushed a soft-bristled brush down Adam's back, arms, and legs with deep, long strokes to calm his nervous system and allow him to integrate other experiences, Georgia pulled the letters from an envelope and scattered them around Adam's desk. A sharp intake of breath indicated Adam's pleasure at the new alphabet before him.

"Adam. These are the letters for you. You look like you like the feeling." Georgia smiled as Adam grasped each letter between his index finger and thumb, rubbing the sides. She gave Adam a quick squeeze around the shoulders before making an announcement to the class. "Friends, today we're working on our names. Find the first letter of your first name." The other students all had an alphabet chart with eight letters, but Adam was working to arrange and rearrange the letters on his desk. Georgia walked by to see that Adam was holding up an "A" for her to see.

"Yes! A for Adam! Great job!" Georgia reached across Adam's desk with her hand up, indicating that she wanted a high five. He'd made such progress since he'd been at GLS, working with his occupational therapist and speech therapist three times a week in addition to school five days a week. Together, they'd all worked on developing his vocabulary by increasing his understanding of familiar picture icons. Through increasing his communication through visual support, including objects and picture symbols, and increasing his regulation through swinging, the weighted blanket for ten minutes each hour, and the skin brushing, Adam's tantrums diminished greatly. Except one. Each day for three months, he had a full-on violent outburst in the cafeteria at lunchtime. As the clock ticked ever closer to noon, Georgia started becoming anxious. She had looked at the antecedent-behavior-consequence pattern and tried several approaches that just weren't working.

"Friends, let's wash hands," she called out to her class. As they lined up, she took Adam's hands in her own and guided him to turn on the faucet, push the soap container, and then scrub his hands as the warm water washed over them. Afterwards, the class lined up in the hallway, and as soon as Georgia opened the door to the cafeteria, Adam flung himself to the ground and screamed.

"No!" Adam yelled. Thud, thud. Georgia could feel the vibrations of Adam's head hitting the cold tile floor. Tim used physical intervention to prevent Adam from self-harm. Adam bucked Tim, slamming his head back into the ground and crying out "No!" with even more fervor than before. He threw his head toward Tim, a blow that he adeptly avoided as he pulled Adam back into his arms.

Tim used physical intervention, holding him tightly. After a few minutes of squirming, thrashing, and attempting self-harm and aggression, Adam calmed. Tim released him to sit calmly on the floor first and then led Adam to in a chair in the dining room. A residual hiccup from his cries escaped his chest as he finally rose with Tim to walk to the lunch line.

Georgia collected herself and realized that her anxiety was misplaced. As she picked over the salad she'd packed herself for lunch, she realized that Adam's meltdown had become part of his routine. She needed to establish a new routine—and fast. That afternoon, when the other students were having a rest hour, Georgia collected Adam and checked out a camera from the main office. She led Adam into the cafeteria, and just as he started to shift his weight between his feet, she pulled out the camera.

"Adam, stand here. I will take your picture." Georgia stood him in front of the door.

He proudly strutted over to the double doors of the cafeteria.

"Say 'cheese'!" Georgia smiled.

"Cheese!" he exclaimed, a big grin breaking across his face.

"Very good! Big smile! Go inside?" Georgia coaxed.

Adam turned and walked ahead of Georgia, where she had Grace, a food service employee, waiting behind the buffet line as though she were distributing food.

"Adam, hold your tray. Smile with Grace?"

Adam grabbed the tray and turned back to Georgia. "Cheeeeeeeeese!" He drew it out and smiled even bigger this time. Georgia took Adam through all the steps of the lunch experience with no meltdown. She even had Grace procure some crackers so that Adam could have a snack. He gobbled them down greedily and giggled. Georgia walked Adam back up to his room, where Tim was waiting.

The next morning, before lunch, Georgia pulled out what she'd worked on for the better part of an hour after school. She put the package on Adam's desk before him.

"Adam, let's read this book," Georgia said cheerfully as she took a seat next to him.

When she opened the first page, Adam giggled excitedly.

The picture of his smiling face at the cafeteria door greeted them.

"Adam, this book is about you!" Georgia said. She began to read, "When I go to lunch, I walk in with my class and wait calmly and happily in line."

She turned the page. "When I go through the line, I will let the staff know what I want to eat. They are here to help me choose my meal. I then go get my silverware and have a seat at the table to eat my food. If I feel mad, all I have to do is say 'Mad' and someone will bring me a glass of water that I can drink because that is what is nice. If I want more food, I go back and stand quietly at the end of the line again. I eat my food, and I feel happy! My teacher and staff also feel happy!" Georgia continued to read the book to Adam, and when they were done, she looked up at his beaming face.

"This story is special because it is about you. This is what we do when we go down to the cafeteria to eat lunch. This is your book!"

"Me?" Adam held the book to his chest.

"Yes. We will read it again each day before lunch."

Adam smiled and rose to stand by the sink. He was ready to wash his hands and go to the cafeteria.

CHAPTER 33
MAMA'S COOKING

"Hello, my big boy! I'm so happy to see you!" Elena walked into Adam's dorm room where he was waiting with Will on his bed.

"He won't do anything except sit here with his suitcase." Will was smiling. "I think he's excited to see you."

Adam began flapping his arms when he heard his mother's voice. He jumped up and hugged her, picking her up off her feet.

"I'm happy to see you, too, big boy! Are you ready to go home?" Elena asked, stroking the side of his face.

"He's been averaging about seven hours of sleep a night," Will said. "I'll miss you, buddy. Have a good visit and I'll see you Monday."

"Oh! I almost forgot." Will turned to Adam's desk and handed Elena a stack of papers. "Ms. Georgia wanted to give you this. Adam made it for you."

Elena flipped through the papers to see artwork, including a watercolor painting of four stick figures holding chicken legs.

"Is this us?" she asked Adam, who nodded and giggled.

"It's wonderful, Adam! Thank you!" Elena was genuinely touched. She'd never had anything tangible that indicated Adam thought of her when she wasn't around. "Let's get going. I'm going to cook fried chicken tonight."

"Nothing better than your mama's cooking, buddy. Enjoy." Will waved as he led them out of the room.

CHAPTER 34
FAMILY CUDDLE

"Would you like more chicken, Adam?" Elena asked her son, offering him the platter as he grabbed three more pieces. "No one's going to take it away, sweetie. Enjoy it." Adam's contagious laughter spread across the table until they were all wiping tears from their eyes. No one knew exactly what was so funny—they were just relieved to be together.

"I hope you had a good week, Adam." Shannon said.

Adam smiled at her.

"I'm so happy you're home," Jon said. "I love you."

Adam reached over and took his father's hand, which he held while he ate the last three pieces of fried chicken.

After dinner, Elena filled the garden tub in the master bathroom with bubbles and pulled out all of Adam's toy boats. She laughed at his arm flapping and giggles when he saw the tub waiting for him, and he scrambled to pull off his shorts. Once he was in, she sat on the side, working around his play to lather up his hair with the lavender shampoo that she'd used on him since he was little. The aroma filled the bathroom, along with the splashing of the water and the collision of the plastic boats. Elena started singing choruses of "Row, Row, Row Your Boat." Adam was beside himself with laughter and tried to join in, making noises in tune with the melody.

Elena was finally able to pull Adam from the tub after three refills of hot water. She helped him get into his flannel pajama bottoms and a t-shirt, and the two of them met Jon and Shannon on the king-sized bed.

"Family cuddle!" Shannon exclaimed. "We haven't done this since we were kids. I remember doing this on Adam's first birthday. We piled into your bed and watched cartoons."

Elena's eyes misted at the memory. On Monday, they would have to return Adam to school, and the next week, she and Jon were driving Shannon to Evanston, where she'd begin her life as a college student. "It all went by so fast, didn't it, Jon?"

Jon smiled, the corners of his eyes crinkling and revealing that he'd most recently passed his fortieth birthday. "It did." He leaned into his wife, with his daughter on his other side and Adam resting his head between his parents. They all settled into their positions in the bed—in the family. Elena smelled the lavender shampoo wafting up from Adam's still damp hair when he turned up to her. For several seconds, he looked her in the eyes, and her breath caught in her chest. It was that look of recognition he'd so rarely given her as a baby, his big brown eyes reaching for the meaning he attached to her face. She saw everything click for him as he leaned toward her and said, barely above a whisper, "Mim."

HOW THESE BOOKS WERE CREATED

The ORP Library of disabilities books is the result of heartfelt collaboration between numerous people: the staff of ORP, including the CEO, executive director, psychologists, clinical coordinators, teachers, and more; the families of children with disabilities served by ORP, including some of the children themselves; and the Round Table Companies (RTC) storytelling team. To create these books, RTC conducted dozens of intensive, intimate interviews over a period of months and performed independent research in order to truthfully and accurately depict the lives of these families. We are grateful to all those who donated their time in support of this message, generously sharing their experience, wisdom, and—most importantly—their stories so that the books will ring true. While each story is fictional and not based on any one family or child, we could not have envisioned the world through their eyes without the access we were so lovingly given. It is our hope that in reading this uniquely personal book, you felt the spirit of everyone who contributed to its creation.

ACKNOWLEDGMENTS

The authors would like to thank the following team members at Genesee Lake School and ORP who generously lent their time and expertise to this book: clinical coordinator Eric Fleischmann, occupational therapists Tracy Hoffman and Gus Ludwig, ICARE program coordinator Jim Lynch, speech and language pathologist Cheryl Norstrem, program supervisors Tony Pierson and Dan Staffin, and special education teacher Emily Richter. Your passion, experience, and wisdom make this book an invaluable tool for other educators, families, and therapists. Thank you for your enthusiastic contributions to this project.

We would also like to extend our heartfelt gratitude to the families who shared their journeys with us. To the Sam Haas family; to Amy, David, Emily, and Andrew Metz; to Linda Rose and her little angel, Hannah; and to Bridgitt and Kevin Montijo, parents of Kyle—thank you for letting us into your worlds, for sharing with us so openly your times of worry, fear, desperation, determination, love, and hope. The courage, ferocity, and love with which you shepherd your children through their lives is nothing short of heroic. You are the reason this book exists.

And to readers of Mr. Incredible—the parents committed to helping their children, the educators who teach those children skills needed for greater independence, the therapists who shine a light on what can be a frighteningly mysterious road, and the schools and counties that make difficult financial decisions to benefit these children: thank you. Your work is miraculous.

JEFFREY D. KRUKAR, PH.D.

BIOGRAPHY

Jeffrey D. Krukar, Ph.D. is a licensed psychologist and certified school psychologist with more than 20 years of experience working with children and families in a variety of settings, including community based group homes, vocational rehabilitation services, residential treatment, juvenile corrections, public schools, and private practice. He earned his Ph.D. in educational psychology, with a school psychology specialization and psychology minor, from the University of Wisconsin-Milwaukee. Dr. Krukar is a registrant of the National Register of Health Service Providers in Psychology, and is also a member of the American Psychological Association.

As the psychologist at Genesee Lake School in Oconomowoc, WI, Dr. Krukar believes it truly takes a village to raise a child—to strengthen developmental foundations in relating, communicating, and thinking—so they can successfully return to their families and communities. Dr. Krukar hopes the ORP Library of disabilities books will bring to light the stories of children and families to a world that is generally not aware of their challenges and successes, as well as offer a sense of hope to those currently on this journey. His deepest hope is that some of the concepts in these books resonate with parents and professionals working with kids with disabilities, and offer possibilities that will help kids achieve their maximum potential and life enjoyment.

CHELSEA McCUTCHIN

BIOGRAPHY

Chelsea McCutchin believes that the transformative power of story is what has bound us together as humanity for ages. She is blessed to work with Round Table Companies, Inc. as a staff editor. This is her first novel project, and she is humbled to be the vessel relaying the challenges and triumphs of families of children with autism spectrum disorder. Chelsea studied English and creative writing at the University of Texas at Austin, and when she isn't writing can be found with her supportive husband, Matt, and their amazing son, Jackson, in her home state of Florida.

JAMES G. BALESTRIERI

BIOGRAPHY

James G. Balestrieri is currently the CEO of Oconomowoc Residential Programs, Inc. (ORP). He has worked in the human services field for 40 years, holding positions that run the gamut to include assistant maintenance, assistant cook, direct care worker, teacher's aide, summer camp counselor, bookkeeper, business administrator, marketing director, CFO, and CEO. Jim graduated from Marquette University with a B.S. in Business Administration (1977) and a Master's in Business Administration with an emphasis in Marketing (1988). He is also a Certified Public Accountant (Wisconsin—1982). Jim has a passion for creatively addressing the needs of those with impairments by managing the inherent stress among funding, programming, and profitability. He believes that those with a disability enjoy rights and protections that were created by the hard-fought efforts of those who came before them; that the Civil Rights movement is not just for minority groups; and that people with disabilities have a right to find their place in the world and to achieve their maximum potential as individuals. For more information, see *www.orp.com*.

ABOUT ORP

Oconomowoc Residential Programs, Inc. is an employee-owned family of companies whose mission is to make a difference in the lives of people with disabilities. Our dedicated staff of 2,000 employee owners provides quality services and professional care to more than 1,700 children, adolescents, and adults with special needs. ORP provides a continuum of care, including residential therapeutic education, community-based residential services, support services, respite care, treatment programs, and day services. The individuals in our care include people with developmental disabilities, physical disabilities, and intellectual disabilities. **Our guiding principle is passion:** a passion for the people we serve and for the work we do. For a comprehensive look at our programs and people, please visit *www.orp.com*.

ORP offers two residential therapeutic education programs and one alternative day school among its array of services. These programs offer developmentally appropriate education and treatment for children, adolescents and young adults in settings specially attuned to their needs. We provide special programs for students with specific academic and social issues relative to a wide range of disabilities, including autistic disorder, Asperger's disorder, mental retardation, anxiety disorders, depression, bipolar disorder, reactive attachment disorder, attention deficit disorder, Prader-Willi syndrome, and other disabilities.

Genesee Lake School is a nationally recognized provider of comprehensive residential treatment, educational, and vocational services for children, adolescents, and young adults with emotional, mental health, neurological, or developmental disabilities. GLS has specific expertise in Autism Spectrum Disorders, anxiety and mood disorders, and behavioral disorders. We provide an individualized, person-centered, integrated team approach, which emphasizes positive behavioral support, therapeutic relationships, and developmentally appropriate practices. Our goal is to assist each individual to acquire skills to live, learn, and succeed in a community-based, less restrictive environment. GLS is particularly known for its high quality educational services for residential and day school students.

Genesee Lake School / Admissions Director
36100 Genesee Lake Road
Oconomowoc, WI 53066
262-569-5510
http://www.geneseelakeschool.com

T.C. Harris School is located in an attractive setting in Lafayette, Indiana. T.C. Harris teaches skills to last a lifetime, through a full therapeutic program as well as day school and other services.

T.C. Harris School / Admissions Director
3700 Rome Drive
Lafayette, IN 47905
765-448-4220
http://tcharrisschool.com

The Richardson School is a day school in West Allis, Wisconsin that provides an effective, positive alternative education environment serving children from Milwaukee and the surrounding communities.

The Richardson School / Director
6753 West Roger Street
West Allis, WI 53219
414-540-8500
http://www.richardsonschool.com

RESOURCES

American Psychiatric Association. *Diagnostic and Statistical Manual of Mental Disorders, Fourth Edition, Text Revision.* Washington, DC: American Psychiatric Association, 2000.

Ayres, A. Jean. *Sensory Integration and the Child, 25th Anniversary Edition: Understanding Hidden Sensory Challenges.* Los Angeles, CA: Western Psychological Services, 2005.

Baker, Jed. *No More Meltdowns: Positive Strategies for Managing and Preventing Out-of-Control Behavior.* Arlington, TX: Future Horizons, 2008.

Biel, Lindsey, and Peske, Nancy. *Raising a Sensory Smart Child: The Definitive Handbook for Helping Your Child With Sensory Processing Issues.* New York, NY: Penguin Group, 2009.

Frost, Lori, and Bondy, Andy. *The Picture Exchange Communication System Training Manual.* Cherry Hill, NJ: Pyramid Educational Consultants, Inc., 2002.

Greenspan, Stanley, and Wieder, Serena. *The Child with Special Needs: Encouraging Intellectual and Emotional Growth.* Cambridge, MA: Da Capo Press, 1998.

Greenspan, Stanley, and Wieder, Serena. *Engaging Autism: Using the Floortime Approach to Help Children Relate, Communicate, and Think.* Cambridge, MA.: Da Capo Press, 2006.

Hodgdon, L.inda. *Visual Strategies for Improving Communication.* Troy, MI: Quirk Roberts Publishing, 1995.

Reed, Penny. *Designing Environments for Successful Kids: A Resource Manual.* Oshkosh, WI: Wisconsin Assistive Technology Initiative, 2003.

"Autism Internet Modules," *http://www.autisminternetmodules.org.*

"Interdisciplinary Council on Developmental and Learning Disorders," *http://www.icdl.com.*

"IDEA – Building the Legacy: IDEA 2004," *http://idea.ed.gov.*

AUTISM SPECTRUM DISORDER

Mr. Incredible shares the fictional story of Adam, a boy diagnosed with autistic disorder. On Adam's first birthday, his mother recognizes that something is different about him: he recoils from the touch of his family, preferring to accept physical contact only in the cool water of the family's pool. As Adam grows older, he avoids eye contact, is largely nonverbal, and has very specific ways of getting through the day; when those habits are disrupted, intense meltdowns and self-harmful behavior follow. From seeking a diagnosis to advocating for special education services, from keeping Adam safe to discovering his strengths, his family becomes his biggest champion. The journey to realizing Adam's potential isn't easy, but with hope, love, and the right tools and teammates, they find that Adam truly is *Mr. Incredible*. The companion comic in this series, inspired by social stories, offers an innovative, dynamic way to guide children—and parents, educators, and caregivers—through some of the daily struggles experienced by those with autism.

MR. INCREDIBLE

A STORY ABOUT AUTISM,
OVERCOMING CHALLENGING
BEHAVIOR, AND A FAMILY'S FIGHT
FOR SPECIAL EDUCATION RIGHTS

MR. INCREDIBLE

CHILDREN'S COMIC BOOK

ASPERGER'S DISORDER

Meltdown and its companion comic book, *Melting Down*, are both based on the fictional story of Benjamin, a boy diagnosed with Asperger's disorder and additional challenging behavior. From the time Benjamin is a toddler, he and his parents know he is different: he doesn't play with his sister, refuses to make eye contact, and doesn't communicate well with others. And his tantrums are not like normal tantrums; they're meltdowns that will eventually make regular schooling—and day-to-day life—impossible. Both the prose book, intended for parents, educators, and mental health professionals, and the comic for the kids themselves demonstrate that the journey toward hope isn't simple . . . but with the right tools and teammates, it's possible.

MELTDOWN

ASPERGER'S DISORDER,
CHALLENGING BEHAVIOR,
AND A FAMILY'S JOURNEY
TOWARD HOPE

MELTING DOWN

A COMIC FOR KIDS WITH
ASPERGER'S DISORDER AND
CHALLENGING BEHAVIOR

REACTIVE ATTACHMENT DISORDER

An Unlikely Trust: Alina's Story of Adoption, Complex Trauma, Healing, and Hope, and its companion children's book, *Alina's Story*, share the journey of Alina, a young girl adopted from Russia. After living in an orphanage during her early life, Alina is unequipped to cope with the complexities of the outside world. She has a deep mistrust of others and finds it difficult to talk about her feelings. When she is frightened, overwhelmed, or confused, she lashes out in rages that scare her family. Alina's parents know she needs help and work endlessly to find it for her, eventually discovering a special school that will teach Alina new skills. Slowly, Alina gets better at expressing her feelings and solving problems. For the first time in her life, she realizes she is truly safe and loved . . . and capable of loving in return.

AN UNLIKELY TRUST

ALINA'S STORY OF ADOPTION, COMPLEX TRAUMA, HEALING, AND HOPE

ALINA'S STORY

LEARNING HOW TO TRUST, HEAL, AND HOPE

Also look for books on bullying and Prader-Willi syndrome coming soon!

CPSIA information can be obtained at www.ICGtesting.com
Printed in the USA
LVOW121702050513

332060LV00001B/1/P